Your Zodiac Soul

'The depth of John Wadsworth's experiential knowledge shines through this book. It is so refreshing to find the zodiac signs delineated in the old way, as a process of alchemical transformation and soul-growth rather than mere indications of 'character'. The practical format and John's deft touch with language gently leads the reader through profound self-enquiry into en-lighten-ment. Literally shining a light into the parts of our being rarely approached before. Such a joy.'

Judy Hall, author of *The Astrology Bible* and the million-copy-selling *The Crystal Bible*

'In this compelling exploration of the zodiac, experiential astrologer John Wadsworth shares a lifetime of insights that'll help each sign discover the best pathways to self-actualisation and emotional well-being. *Your Zodiac Soul* is an inspired book written with enthusiasm, freshness and passion.'

Frank Clifford, Principal of the London School of Astrology and author of numerous books, including *Getting to the Heart of Your Chart*

'Whether you are new to astrology or a seasoned "pro", this gem of a book will refer you directly to a vision of wholeness which is indigenous to the human soul, connecting you to the Cosmos via the symbols of the zodiac. The "medicine wheel" of the twelve signs is here richly evoked by interwoven mythological themes, and your guide is someone who has for many years travelled this sacred journey experientially as well as intellectually.'

Melanie Reinhart, author of *Chiron and the Healing Journey*

'John Wadsworth's zodiacal tour breaks new ground, elegantly presenting the zodiac both as twelve archetypal gateways and simultaneously as a unified twelve-fold system that can guide one's self-inquiry to personal self-realisation. With skill he weaves a tapestry of wisdom drawing from astrological tradition, myth, history, poetry and literature. Beginners and advanced students will benefit from this book which could have a profound impact upon the reader as an evolutionary tool.'

Martin Davis, author of *Astrolocality Astrology* and *From Here to There*

'With keen mythopoetic understanding, John Wadsworth's *Your Zodiac Soul* revisions astrology as an experiential journey, transiting through twelve portals or stages of initiation. The perspective is constructive, soul-centred rather than character-centred, and Wadsworth is most interested in the soul's task to render mere events into meaningful experiences. He imagines the zodiac as a dynamic wheel of life showing each soul its own unique, mythic transformative path. *Your Zodiac Soul* is also beautifully written, sure to add a deepening clarity for beginners and old hands alike, a pleasure to read, a generous share.'

Jeremiah Abrams, Jungian therapist and author of
Meeting the Shadow and *Reclaiming the Inner Child*

'*Your Zodiac Soul* is an experiential rather than a theoretical vision of astrology. Here John Wadsworth has created a book that will take you on a journey. Accept that invitation sincerely and you will change your life.'

Mark Jones, founder of the Pluto School of Astrology
and author of *Healing the Soul* and *The Souls Speaks*

'A lyrical love letter to the power and subtlety of the zodiac, *Your Zodiac Soul* offers a brand-new approach to anyone interested in personal development, finding more wholeness in their life or expanding their awareness of the influence of the cosmos on our individuality. Based on his extensive experience as an astrologer and facilitator of courses, John Wadsworth invites intuition, imagination and inspiration into our connection with the zodiac and opens gateways to enhanced personal understanding.'

Sue Hollingsworth, Director of the Centre for Biographical Storytellers, coach, consultant and co-author of *The Storyteller's Way*

'John's deeply passionate engagement with our innate connection to the land, the seasons and the stars weaves itself poetically into this magical offering: enchanting us with myths, embedding the pages with a treasure trove of visceral wisdom and offering us a sacred journey of self-discovery. The path between these pages takes us deep into the very fabric of our lives, right to the soul of who we are, opening the locked doors of our hearts and revealing the way to find our own ensouled becoming. It is a profound gift.'

Suzanne Corbie, Tarot consultant and teacher

To Isa,

Enjoy the journey!

With love & blessings,

John

Your Zodiac Soul

Working with the Twelve Zodiac Gateways to Create Balance, Happiness and Wholeness

JOHN WADSWORTH

S

First published in Great Britain in 2018 by Orion Spring
an imprint of The Orion Publishing Group Ltd
Carmelite House, 50 Victoria Embankment
London EC4Y 0DZ

An Hachette UK Company

1 3 5 7 9 10 8 6 4 2

'Fire Hazard', poem by Dorsha Hayes in: Dorsha Hayes, *The Bell Branch Rings*
by kind permission of Bauhans Publishing: Peterborough, NH, 1972.

A CIP catalogue record for this book is
available from the British Library.

ISBN (Trade Paperback) 9781841882819

ISBN (eBook) 9781841882826

Cover illustration: Yuri Leitch
Internal illustrations: Dan Goodfellow

Typeset by Richard Carr
Printed in Great Britain by Clays Ltd, St Ives plc

MIX
Paper from
responsible sources
FSC® C104740

www.orionbooks.co.uk

ORION
SPRING

For Mum, Graham and Sue,
and to the memory of my dear Dad and my late Grandma
who lived just long enough to see this come together.

Contents

Introduction

Turning the wheel of your zodiac soul

There is a wheel turning in you. It is a wheel of time and a wheel of initiation. It is a wheel of lived experience that is reflected in the cyclical passage of the seasons, and in the play of light and shadow that conditions and shapes your life. It is your own personal imprint of the wheel of star constellations that turn around you every day. It is the wheel of your zodiac soul.

I am passionate about astrology, and for twenty-five years I have been working as a professional astrologer, running a busy consulting practice in the south-west of England. I help people to gain a deeper appreciation of themselves, their relationships and their path in life through exploring the intricate workings of their own natal charts.[1] I am fascinated by how we learn, and I consider astrological knowledge to be a vital aspect of a well-rounded education. It can empower our choices in life and help us express more of our potential as human beings, within the context of a greater-than-human cosmos.

I am born under the Sun sign of Aries, and we Arians are natural pioneers. In 2008 I initiated a way of working with the

twelve-sign zodiac as a twelve-step process of personal transformation and healing. It became known as 'The Alchemical
Journey', a year-long course, following the passage of the Sun
through the zodiac signs, co-facilitated by zodiac researcher
Anthony Thorley and myself. During the nine years it has been
running to date, we have witnessed participants from all walks
of life experience major shifts of perspective that have prompted
many of them to make significant changes to their lives and
some to manifest long-held wishes and dreams.[2] I would like to
share the power of this programme with you here.

A route map of the soul

This is not a typical book about the zodiac. There are many
such titles on the market that emphasise the rich and diverse
personality traits associated with each astrological sign, but here
I want to demonstrate a different approach. Drawing on more
than two thousand years of astrological tradition, I will present
the zodiac as an essential route map of the soul. I believe that
we all carry an imprint of the twelve-sign zodiac in our psyche,
and that each sign carries a powerful teaching, conveyed
through stories and metaphors, each offering a very specific
medicine, or totemic power, that can help to heal the imbalances within us. What I call your zodiac soul is that revelation
of you, in the process of becoming the totality of who you are.
The zodiac presents us with a wheel of life that turns within us
and around us through the four elements – fire, earth, air and
water – and that live in us as inspiration, sensation, thinking

and feeling. A healthy wheel is a turning wheel, one that moves and flows and transforms in rhythm with the ever-changing dynamics of life. There are times, though, when we find it hard to move on and we may struggle to integrate and accept the changing circumstances of our lives and our feelings towards them. We can get trapped in particular perspectives that narrow our field of awareness, and our wheel gets stuck there.

By looking at ourselves through the particular lens of each zodiac sign in turn, we can tend to the cries of the soul. We all have areas of life in which we struggle – whether it is self-worth, a sense of belonging, personal relationships, finances, health, which vocation to follow, or how to best contribute to our community. These all have their place in the wheel and by shifting our perspective towards them, the underlying fears and self-defeating behaviours that drive them can be compassionately transformed. Indeed, they can become the very grit necessary to facilitate our soul's recovery.

Twelve gateways to wholeness

One of the aims of this book is to help you identify where the wheel gets stuck in your own life and how you can get it turning again. Everything turns; our planet turns once every year around the Sun, bringing about the cycle of the seasons on Earth, and once every day on its own axis, giving us day and night. Consequently the Sun, Moon and planets appear to travel in a circular motion above and around us. Those turnings describe an ongoing exchange between light and dark, heat and cold, moisture and dryness that are essential conditioning factors of all life on Earth. And so it is within your zodiac soul, which is your own personal impression of these dynamic interactions. The balance of these exchanges is mixed differently in each person and can be understood better through studying the natal chart drawn up for the moment of your birth. Beyond these differences, what we all share in common, through our zodiac soul, is the capacity to respond to the fluctuating conditions of life, which, despite their apparent complexity, derive their significance entirely from natural and cosmic cycles.

Your Zodiac Soul takes up the ancient pre-Christian idea that this imprint of the wheel that we carry within us is part of our collective heritage, and that if we can learn to master the teachings inherent in each of its twelve dimensions, we might fulfil our potential as human beings, and become powerful manifestors in our lives. Taking each sign in order, from Aries through to Pisces, you will be presented with twelve distinct gateways towards realising your full potential as a human being, as well as twelve aspects of your shadow nature to recognise, accept and transform.

Working with your birthchart

Studying your own birthchart and having an understanding of your own personal astrological make-up can act as an extremely useful guide as you contemplate each stage of the wheel. There are online resources to support the journey at www.yourzodiacsoul.com, with guidance as to where to look in your own chart for further insights into each zodiac gateway, whether through your own study or with the help of a trained astrologer. Studying your birthchart is not essential, though, as you can follow the twelve stages presented here without reference to it.

This approach is a tried-and-tested process of healing and transformation and you certainly don't need to be a student of astrology to benefit from it. What it requires of you most of all is a willingness and commitment to understand yourself better and to be willing to open yourself up to the possibility of who you really are and what you could become.

What is the zodiac? A little basic astronomy

The night sky has always been a source of great inspiration to me, as it rightly should be to all of us. I have spent many evenings under the canopy of night learning to identify the stars and constellations above and understand the motions of the planets through direct observation. For years I have been operating a mobile planetarium for children, teaching them basic astronomy, offering them a perspective on science that is still wedded to an experience of mystery and wonder.

The constellational figures, ancient images preserved in the patterns of the stars, are drawn primarily from the mythology of the ancient Greeks. Twelve of these patterns lie along an imaginary line called the ecliptic, which is the path that the Sun follows when seen against the backdrop of the stars.[3] This apparent motion is caused by the Earth's once-yearly orbit around the Sun; from our perspective, it appears that the Sun is making that journey and the distance that it travels is, more or less, one degree of the 360-degree ecliptic circle each day. Because all the planets lie, more or less, on the same plane of orbit as the Sun, their passages can also be plotted to the ecliptic within a few degrees of latitude. This includes the Moon, which experiences the greatest latitude above and below this line in its monthly rhythm. So, broadly speaking, the Sun, Moon and planets will always be found in one of these twelve constellations of the sky. As the Earth rotates on its axis once every twenty-four hours, all these constellations rotate around us once every day, each one rising and setting in turn. From these constellations we derive the twelve signs of the zodiac, each occupying its own 30-degree segment of the ecliptic circle.[4]

What is the zodiac? A little basic history

Astrology and the development of the zodiac would seem to be a consequence of the first agricultural revolution, the shift from hunter-gathering tribes to farming communities. With the establishment of settlements – fixed centres of belonging – the way that people viewed the heavens around them changed to reflect the new understanding of how and when to plant and cultivate grain and other staple crops. The attributes of the zodiacal images correspond to the experience of an agricultural cycle dictated by seasonal change in northern-hemisphere cultures. Astrology was established first by the Babylonians and later by the Greeks and Romans. The images and meanings of the twelve zodiac signs were settled by the Greeks a few centuries BCE.

The zodiac was established around four key turning points in the year: the two equinoxes, when day and night are equal in length, and the two solstices, which mark the longest and shortest days of the year. These points place the ingress of the Sun into the four cardinal signs of the zodiac; the Spring Equinox belongs to Aries, the Summer Solstice to Cancer, the Autumn Equinox to Libra and the Winter Solstice to Capricorn. The spring signs of Aries, Taurus and Gemini are linked to fertility, prosperity and pollination. The summer signs of Cancer, Leo and Virgo coincide with the fruiting, ripening and harvesting of the crop. The autumn signs of Libra, Scorpio and Sagittarius reflect the withdrawal of nature's bounty as the leaves fall and are composted, nights become longer, and with this there is an increase of spiritual awareness and engagement with the deeper mysteries of life and death. In the winter signs of Capricorn, Aquarius and Pisces, the community takes stock, plans ahead and pulls together its collective wisdom and resources, praying and fasting in preparation for spring's return.

Astrology's survival in the modern world

A major reason for the longevity of astrology is that it embodies a practical understanding of solar, lunar and planetary cycles as an inescapable part of rural life. Countless forms of zodiacal

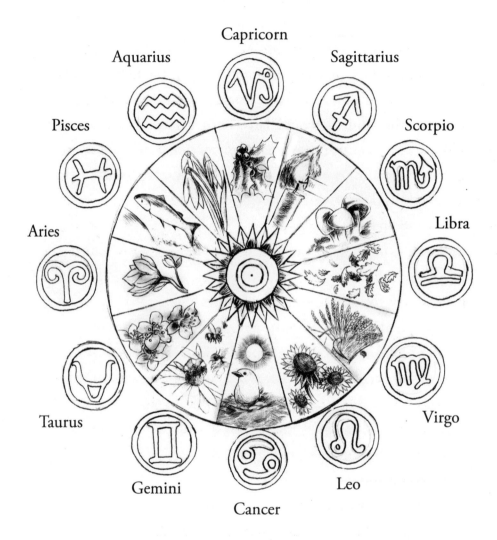

Capricorn

Aquarius

Sagittarius

Pisces

Scorpio

Aries

Libra

Taurus

Virgo

Gemini

Leo

Cancer

calendars found in almanacs attest to this. These calendars helped people to stay connected as a community; the timing of rituals and ceremonies could be established with exactitude by careful observance of the heavens in the days long before clock time had been established as a universal constant. Extending the analogy of planetary cycles to the human body and life cycle is quite natural and logical. For rural folk living close to the land, it would have been a fairly obvious and self-evident fact that the human body grew and flowered, decayed, died and experienced rebirth in much the same way as the rest of the natural world.

From the twelfth century and for the next five hundred years or so, a naturalistic form of astrology was even sanctioned within Roman Catholicism, and the Bible itself is replete with astrological references. Images of the twelve zodiac signs are frequently found in pre-Reformation churches and cathedrals; sometimes the whole zodiac wheel itself is depicted. Physicians from the medieval period were all trained astrologers, and while there always remained a certain tension between the Church and astrology, knowledge of the stars was accepted as part and parcel of medical practice for hundreds of years.

Despite its obvious antiquity, astrology has not had an easy ride, either within religious or secular culture. It sits well below the radar of acceptability in modern society, yet it continues to be a source of popular interest and fascination. Almost everyone knows their Sun sign, and the promise that our destiny could in some way be connected to the stars is ultimately compelling to us. Once a person has started to look, even superficially, at an interpretation of his or her birthchart, they are likely to become hooked. The idea that we can discern meaning in the movements of the heavenly bodies goes right to the core of our belief structures and religious impulses. In Western culture the zodiac wheel itself is the most consistent representation of this, and it is deeply embedded in the collective psyche. And it simply won't go away! Astrology has always found a way to survive, despite being denigrated as a religious heresy, an affront to science or an insult to the educated intellect.[5] Yet it consistently proves its efficacy and delivers real value in practice for those who take the time to study it.

An alchemical journey

I consider working with the zodiac wheel to be alchemical work. Alchemy is a hugely complex subject and I will not attempt to explain its intricate workings here, but when simply understood, it is the art of transformation. It can be thought of as both a study and a practice that can allow direct, experiential access to the regenerative force of creation, the creative genius that continually weaves the web of life.

Alchemy is among the most mysterious of the metaphysical arts. Its tradition is closely interwoven with medicine, astrology and magic and its lore is rich in symbolic understanding. Contained in its fantastic images and poetic aphorisms, one finds profound metaphorical references to plants, minerals, elemental intelligences and planetary bodies. Our modern idea of an alchemist tends to conjure up visions of strangely clad men in primitive laboratories attempting to turn base metal into gold. This seems absurd to our modern ways of thinking, and so alchemy is often dismissed as a pursuit of fools, despite the uncomfortable fact that some rather eminent and progressive scientists, such as Isaac Newton, spent much of their time pursuing it! We moderns tend to see only the outer attempt to change one 'thing' into another 'thing'; in doing so we miss the 'inner', philosophical transformation that must always accompany it.

Alchemy has been described as 'a rainbow bridging the chasm between the earthly and heavenly planes, between matter and spirit', the alchemical texts concealing in their enigmatic symbols 'the means of penetrating the very secrets of Nature, Life, and Death, of Unity, Eternity, and Infinity'.[6] The zodiac has been described as 'an alchemical vessel for the sufferings of psyche',[7] and it can be a magical container where all the psychic jumble, all that dark, fearful, shameful stuff that we hide away from the world, becomes the raw material – *prima materia* – for our transformational process. So the pain and troubles of our lives can be revealed as the very soil from which we emerge transformed, ensouled. Through a ritual imitation of nature's processes, we can grow richer perspectives that enable us to peer through the different veils of reality into the deepest truth of who we are.

A wheel of images

We see the zodiac as a twelve-sign circle consisting of mainly animal representations (the word zodiac translates as 'a circle of animals') that has been depicted with consistency and coherence for over two thousand years in Greek, Roman and late-Egyptian temples, as well as in Christian churches and numerous ancient books, tapestries, paintings and friezes. It has also been preserved as the basis of religious observances and ritual initiations through the myths and stories of mystery traditions from Mithraism to medieval alchemy, each of which has carefully retained the correct order of the figures.[8]

So here we have a wheel of images that is also a turning wheel of time, one deeply embedded in the collective psyche as calendrical marker, astrological map, alchemical vessel and cyclical narrative for the mystery school initiate. The zodiac offers us a series of root archetypes that provide the contextual fabric for all our human experiences. By allowing its mysteries to unfold in our imaginations, it can activate deep longings for connection to a realm of wisdom that we have temporarily forgotten. And once that realm has been glimpsed, it can hold a fascination for us, as it draws us further into the mystery of who we are and who we might become. By donning the mask of each zodiac sign, learning to see through the eyes of each in turn, and embodying its archetypal energy, we can rediscover aspects of ourselves that we have neglected or overlooked. Furthermore, we become better able to accept things about ourselves and others that we might previously have found intolerable.

The zodiac as a twelve-stage process of transformation

The main focus of this book is to elaborate on each of the twelve stages of the wheel, exploring the possibilities and challenges that confront us at each step along the way. Let me whet your appetite for what is to come with a brief sketch of each sign's manifesting potential. Aries gives us the power of intention, Taurus the blessing of gratitude, Gemini the ability to communicate and articulate what we want to bring about. Cancer connects us to the deep treasure chest of our innermost feelings, Leo to our confidence and creativity, Virgo to our capacity to cultivate and harvest our dreams through practice and daily observance. Libra brings us into relationship and brings balance and proportion to our desires, while Scorpio confronts us with their shadow aspect and compels us to look within, to the deeper implications of who we are and what we want. Sagittarius lifts us and inspires a higher vision of what is possible for our lives, while Capricorn tests that in reality, strengthening our purpose and commitment. Aquarius inspires us with an enlightening overview so that we might consider our own dreams and wishes within the context of the wider communities to which we belong and in service to them. And finally, Pisces opens our mystic eye, enabling us to feel into the true boundless depth of our connectedness as soul beings.

Encountering the shadow energy of each sign

This all sounds wonderful, doesn't it? Well, if only it were that easy, we would all be living our dreams and manifesting our highest potential at will. The issue, as we shall see in the ensuing chapters, is that it takes courage, tenacity, intelligence and emotional receptivity to bring this to reality. And we need to actively employ these qualities in order to address the shadow aspect of each zodiac sign as we journey around the wheel. This 'shadow energy', as I will refer to it from now on, seems to work against our highest potential and can undermine, even sabotage, our best intentions. So the real work is in becoming more aware of these tendencies at each stage of the wheel, noticing where they trip us up and hinder our progress. As we will see, our job is not to banish this 'shadow energy' but to accept it, integrate it into our awareness and gradually coax out its hidden transforming power.

Shadow energy: Aries to Virgo

In Aries, we find the courage to take a risk and begin, but we must beware of being too impulsive or aggressive in pursuit of our desires, or giving up too easily when things don't immediately go our way. In Taurus, our task is to accept and appreciate the good things that life has to offer but, in the midst of such abundance, to be wary of greed and the tendency to hold on too tightly to what we have for fear of losing it. Gemini offers many bright and enchanting opportunities to be grasped with the keenness of our wits, but fickleness, impatience, loose talk and instability can be our undoing here. If we can trust our intuitive feelings, Cancer offers us sanctuary, nurture and deep connection, but the longing for home and emotional security can make us fearful and overprotective; we might just disappear into our shell, never to be seen again! While Leo graces us with the realisation of the creative power within each of us, we must also find the courage to express that, and we can come unstuck through excessive pride and arrogance, making ourselves too central to everything around us. In Virgo, we get to the real work of manifestation and must be prepared to apply ourselves in some form of regular practice; but we can also get too pedantic, overly critical or small-minded at this stage.

Shadow energy: Libra to Pisces

As we progress into the second half of the wheel and are reminded of the balance in all things, Libra invites us into the blessing of relationship; but if we vacillate, compromise too much or try too hard to overaccommodate another person's needs, we risk losing the authenticity of our true nature. Scorpio seeks emotional commitment and a ruthless desire for the truth which hides itself away in dark places, but when we are overly suspicious of whatever is within and around us, we become our own worst enemy. In Sagittarius we need the courage to adventure beyond the far horizon. Fuelled with inspiration and renewed faith, we seek the meaning of life; but we can be clumsy, tactless and self-righteous, even fanatical in our spiritual or religious beliefs. Capricorn calls us to commit to our authentic vocation in life, but in order to do that we must face our unease around authority, the feeling of being trapped in a system that controls us or being overly controlling in the way in which we wield our own authority. Next, our Aquarian intelligence and social awareness is called for so that we might perceive the highest potential for all and recognise the unique contribution that we make to the world. But a certain aloofness from the human experience can render us cold, brittle and apparently lacking in compassion. And in Pisces we drop again into the realm of deep feelings and the realisation of how deeply connected we are to each other and to the Universe. But as we dive deeper into this sublime knowing, we can become dis-integrated from material reality, deluded, lost, addicted to anything which promises escape from the world with all its suffering.

An invitation to the journey

The zodiac offers us twelve stages of initiation on the way to becoming a more complete, more aware, more compassionate human being. Our main access to the signs of the zodiac, within mainstream culture at least, is through what we know and experience about the traits of people born with the Sun in each demarcated sector of the tropical zodiac.[9] The recognition of those traits will be a useful touchstone as we progress through the chapters of this book. Resist the temptation to jump ahead to the chapters that relate to your own Sun sign or those of the people in your life, though, as this book is not structured along the lines of character delineation. Instead, it is designed so that you will meet each sign in turn, in their correct order, and each will offer up to you a perspective on the world. Some will be more familiar and some will feel more comfortable than others. Dwell a little longer on the ones that you react against, or that seem foreign to you, as these may have the most to teach you.

Myths, gods and archetypes

I have always found that the most effective way to understand astrology and really get to grips with its complex dynamics is through the medium of myth. Planets and stars have long been identified as gods, the characters that populate our mythology in all cultures of the world. These powerful, other-than-human deities were recognised as having a major part to play in the functioning of everyday life. The planets being gods, their signs were recognised through correlations with cycles of everyday life by astronomer-priests who closely observed them and made interpretations based upon their appearance, their placements in relation to one another and the characteristic nature of their motions. The roots of astrology lie in a pre-Christian cosmology where the gods were numerous and complex in character, each ruling over a different aspect of life. Offerings, also known as sacrifices, were made at appropriate and auspicious times in order to solicit particular deities, in the hope of gaining their favour.

Astrology confronts us with a pantheon of deities, each demanding different things from us. Nowadays we speak of the presence of the gods in our lives more through the psychological notion of archetypes, a term popularised by C.G. Jung, who spoke of a collective unconscious which guides our thoughts, actions and behaviours. Within this realm lie a complex array of archetypes, each with their own characteristics, each an essential part of what makes us who we are. Jung emphasised the need to integrate each of these into the Self in order to achieve a healthy functioning psyche. Having a passionate interest in astrology himself, he considered that 'the planets are the gods, symbols of the powers of the unconscious'.[10] Thus the astrological symbol becomes a metaphor carrying archetypal meaning, discernible through the stories of the gods. The nature of symbols was of prime concern to Jung, their meaning extending far beyond a mere linguistic association. He saw symbols as participatory powers, possessed of complex agency, capable of opening us up to the realm of the mythic.

Mythic time

Myth deals in cycles, and stories that populate the mythic realm exist outside of, and beyond, historical linear time. They may or may not ever have happened in historical time, but they live within our imaginations in such a way that we can access their power and meaning. A mythic beginning returns us to our origins so that we might recreate those same conditions and apply them metaphorically within the time span of our own lives, what Mircea Eliade called the 'eternal return'.[11] We can, for example, engage imaginatively with the cycle of a creation myth at any point in our lives that may constitute a new beginning, such as when a parent dies, when a relationship ends, when we lose our job, or when we have to recreate a new sense of who we are and what our lives mean.

A cyclical rendering of time can be reassuring, nurturing, strengthening, and can help us to trust our embodied experience of ourselves and the world. Time conceived as a straight line is abstract, distant, disembodied, stress-inducing; it is counter to our body's daily and monthly rhythms, counter to our experience of the seasons, and to our lived experience of being in the world. In the zodiac, our beginning point is Aries, but this doesn't arise out of nowhere. It follows on from Pisces, the last sign, where we forget who we are as a separate entity and unite with the oneness of all beings. Yet strong Aries types often behave as if they are creating new things from nothing. Children have to learn to do everything from scratch, but they are also drawing on the aeons of collective experience of those who have gone through this before.

The zodiac as round table

The pluralistic nature of myth is reflected in the zodiac's range of twelve unique and integral perspectives of the world that together form a complete assembly. This is analogous to the twelve gods and goddesses of Mount Olympus, the twelve labours of Hercules, the twelve tribes of Israel, the twelve apostles, and so on. In some versions of the legend, it was also considered that there were twelve places at the Round Table of King Arthur; for our purposes here, this is a compelling notion. Twelve unique perspectives, integrated in the round, present as part of an archetypal structure within each one of us. This round-table gathering honours the particular contribution and difference that each member makes and celebrates their common ground as an interconnected fellowship, subject to the order of nature and cosmos. Such an appreciation breeds tolerance, compassion and the realisation that we are all working towards a common goal. At a round table every seat is the head place, the all committed to the one, and the one to the all. This is a very healthy model for any community, and it can serve the same restorative function with the human psyche.

Before we get too comfortable with this, it should be stated that in most cultural systems, and zodiacs, there is also a thirteenth member who breaks up the neat solar symmetry of the twelve: a wilder, lunar member who remembers the thirteen moons of the year. She is uninvited to the solar assembly, rejected or outcast. She is the grit in the wheel and her removal sits uncomfortably in the psyche. The memory of her banishment serves as a continual reminder that a vital aspect of the feminine has been excluded. We have inherited a zodiac with a patriarchal bias and there is a need to restore the integrity of the female perspective in some, if not all, of the zodiac signs. We will meet her at particular key points on the journey.

The zodiac as medicine wheel

Think of the zodiac as a medicine wheel with the myths of each sign carrying archetypal powers, which offer a healing balm to address the painful sense of being separated from our origins, a wound that lies deep in the psyche. Myths offer a particular kind of medicine for the soul. As we progress around the wheel we can imagine that we are exposing ourselves to that story medicine, embodying its teachings, imbibing its often bitter tonic, inhabiting the qualities it bestows. To restore ourselves to full health and well-being, we need to integrate each one of these recuperative myths into our awareness in appreciation of the order in which they occur in the cyclical round. A myth has the ability to take us out from the place that we think we know and show us a new perspective. It can make us aware of what we don't know, help us break a pattern that is limiting our ability to know, and then return us to where we began so that we might see that same situation through different eyes.

Synchronicity as a paradigm

Myths cross the borders between the inner (unmanifest) and the outer (manifest) dimensions of reality. The relationship between a person's soul and their outward fate is mythic; when astrological symbolism is understood within this context, experience shifts towards a paradigm of what Jung called synchronicity, the meaningful coincidence of one's inner and outer reality: '…the coincidence of events in space and time as meaning something more than mere chance, namely, a peculiar interdependence of objective events among themselves as well as with the subjective (psychic) states of the observer or observers'.[12]

As you take this journey and engage with the deeply storied zodiac you will be seeding your imagination with new possibilities; as you do so, you might start to notice connections between things that you encounter in your life that you hadn't seen before. Meaningful coincidences will become more apparent, and you might even begin to sense that you are being guided by the signs that appear. If you do, follow these signs and see where they lead you. This is a powerful exercise in reconnecting with your deep soul and there are many untapped riches there, just waiting to be discovered.

Encountering the myths of each zodiac sign

As we encounter each sign in the following chapters we will meet different mythic characters and themes that exemplify that sign and their stories will offer you powerful keys to reconnect you to your zodiac soul. In Aries we encounter a golden ram who saved a young boy from the blind conviction of his father, and carried him off to begin an adventure of his own. In Taurus we meet the Minotaur and face the consequences of coveting what we love too exclusively. In Libra we are led to the scales of Ma'at, where the heart is weighed against her feather. Then there are the stories of the

planetary deities who rule over the zodiac signs, whose
adventures offer us deep insights in the nature of each
zodiacal energy as we seek to integrate each one in turn on
our journey. There are also stories related to the time of year
in which each sign falls, seasonal cues that perfectly capture
its spirit and meaning.

A good story is not always a comfortable one. It will deliver
meaning on more than one level, sometimes in ways that are
not easily palatable. Myths often feature characters (human
and animal) that are grotesque in nature, or act in ways that
are excessively violent or amoral. Such stories speak to the
soul, and we are unsettled by them; they challenge our
domestic equilibrium, stir us out of our complacency, take us
beyond what we know. The soul can be a place of exquisite
beauty but it can also be a battleground; it is where we meet
our shadow nature. A journey like this does not promise
one-stop solutions or salvation, but it does open up new ways
of seeing ourselves and new ways of being.

The mythic also offers us some emotional distance from our
everyday concerns, from the attachments, limitations and
neuroses of our fallible human personalities. As Carl Sagan,
quoting Sallustius, once said, 'myths are things that never
happened, but always are'.[13] They should not be taken literally,
for they are capricious and ambiguous. The attempt to literalise
a myth often leads to fundamentalist beliefs. Myths necessarily
leave room for active imagination, thriving off enquiry and a
creative response capable of hauling them out of the realm of
possibility and into everyday lived reality. As such, they become

powerful agents of manifestation. They are mercurial, shape-shifting, capable of adapting themselves to meet the needs of the situation to which they are called.

The sacred order of twelve

In a rare allusion to the zodiac, Plato once described the Universe as being twelve-sided (dodecahedron) in shape and patterned with animal figures.[14] The zodiacal order of twelve is implicit in the harmonic fabric of creation. Wise elders in society have recognised this for millennia, incorporating it into the design of their kingdoms and communities, expressing it through their traditional songs, stories and celebrations. It presents us with a paradox; not only does it involve the shape-shifting mystery of transformation, it also, according to John Michell and Christine Rhone, constitutes the 'proper foundation of a sacred order'.[15] As they demonstrate in *Twelve-Tribe Nations*, the division of a circle into twelve parts is a pattern that has been consistently detected in the heavens and brought to Earth in the form of landscape zodiacs and twelve-tribe societies. He cites numerous examples of the zodiac acting as an enchantment upon the collective imagination, reminding us of Plato's injunction that people 'must continually hear and repeat the traditional songs, charms and stories, but in constantly changing forms'. Michell and Rhone suggest 'an epic narrative, accompanied by a ceaseless chant which reflects the various episodes of the story, and reflects also the progression of seasons and astrological cycles'.[16]

When people realise this connection, it often inspires a kind of epiphany, a sense of meaningful connectedness, as it reunites people with nature and its cycles. This happened to one of our participants, harpist and songwriter Vicki Burke, during the first year of The Alchemical Journey programme. During our Libra weekend, she suddenly realised that a number of the songs she had written during her career fitted a zodiacal pattern almost perfectly through both their musical style and their lyrical meaning. It occurred to her that she had unwittingly created a repertoire of twelve songs that reflected the twelve signs, corresponding both to the seasonal year and to the different stages of the human life cycle. From this, she crafted a two-hour performance based around these twelve songs, woven through with her new awareness of how these different cycles synchronise symbolically. She has since published a book describing the musical and philosophical journey that it inspired for her.[17] This is one of a number of examples of students who have been inspired by a twelve-fold zodiacal pattern expressed through their creative work.

How to work with this book

A process of self-enquiry

What I present here in this book is a framework for self-enquiry, an opportunity for you to look at the whole of your life from a range of perspectives, drawn from the deep wellspring of zodiacal images and their associated mythology. Prompted by these stories and symbols, there is an invitation here for you to ask deep and searching questions of yourself, and incorporate certain exercises and practices into your life. Think of each zodiac image as an essential part of who you are, each one a gateway of understanding that can bring balance and integrity to twelve different dimensions of your life. There will be some parts of the wheel that you tend to lean on too heavily, and others that you tend to neglect. You will feel this intuitively as you read through the chapters, and it will also likely be reflected in the signatures of your own natal chart. I hope this book will inspire you to want to study your own chart, so that you can work with the twelve gateways alongside it. If you treat this journey with some reverence and take it seriously, it could, and should, change your life in some quite extraordinary ways!

Find a time rhythm that works for you

You can follow the chapters in a time rhythm that suits you. For example, you could follow the annual cycle of the Sun through the signs of the zodiac, as we do on *The Alchemical Journey*, spending a month reading, reflecting and practising with each of the twelve zodiacal stages through the year. The only drawback with this approach is that you would need to start around the time of the Spring Equinox; if you are picking up this book at a different time of year, you would be unnecessarily delayed. So you could start at the point in the year where you are – people have done that on the programme in the past and have still got a lot from the process. But if you're like me, you will want to start at the beginning! So a more realistic option is to work with the monthly lunar cycle. Find out when the Moon goes into Aries and start at that point. Then spend two or three days on each chapter while the Moon is in each zodiac sign. This means you complete the journey within twenty-eight days. If you choose to, you can re-read the book and go through the process again. You might want to do this three times, over a three-month period. That would be very powerful indeed.

If neither of these rhythms quite work for you, you could dedicate twelve weeks to the process and spend a week on each sign. The weekly rhythm is very effective. When I first began taking clients through the journey, we followed this model. If you're so inclined, you could do a fast-track twelve-day programme! If you choose either of the two latter options, I would suggest that you select a meaningful moment to start.

Have a copy of your birthchart to hand

Get a copy of your chart drawn up, if you don't have one already. Familiarise yourself with the planets and zodiac symbols. On the website that accompanies this book there are basic delineations of each planet in sign, house and aspect and an easy guide for you to follow through the zodiacal cycle. See: www.yourzodiacsoul.com. You can use these references to give you extra insights as you progress through each stage of the wheel. Please treat these as a very general guide, because they will *not*, by any means, give you the whole story.

If you prefer, you could consult an astrologer, either at the beginning of the journey or at different stages along the way. I would recommend you speak to someone who is sensitive to the process of deep enquiry with which you are engaged, someone who won't be too definitive in their interpretation of your chart.

Keep a journal

Keep a journal throughout the process and make regular entries at each stage, preferably on a daily basis. Notice what happens in your daily life and your responses to what happens. You may find that your dream life also becomes more vivid, so pay attention to your dreams and keep your journal by your bed so that you can write them down. This will greatly assist you in being able to manifest your intentions. Think of it as your alchemical journal, a place where new perceptions, intuitions and realisations can be recorded, and which will often emerge as they are being written. Nobody else will read what you write, so it can be a place of sanctuary, where you can be totally honest with yourself.

Supporting the journey

Don't rush to the next stage of the wheel too soon, at least not until you have spent some time contemplating the teachings of each sign, and integrating and practising the exercises at the end of each chapter. There is a process of transition as you pass from one zodiac gateway to the next where the focus of the enquiry changes. Structure your time with care, so that you will realistically be able to see the journey through to its conclusion. Treat it as a process of mindful enquiry. Take your time with it, go deep, and seek the support you need along the way. You might want to work with a buddy, someone you trust, and you could both read the book in the same time rhythm. You can be a kind of mirror for each other, offering up your opinions on the self-enquiry questions and supporting each other's accountability with the exercises. Be prepared to look into the more uncomfortable truths that arise for you, and they will! I invite you to take this on and be as honest with yourself as you dare to be. The rewards for doing so will be magnificent.

The First Gateway

Aries

Sun in Aries period: *20/21 March (Spring Equinox) – 19/20 April*

Symbol: *The Ram*

Motivation: *Cardinal/initiating*

Element (Temperament): *Fire*

Ruling planet: *Mars*

Body part ruled: *Head*

Keynote: *Here I am. Let's do this.*

Version of the truth: *Passion is everything and everything is now.*

Medicine: *The courage to begin. The power of intention.*

Shadow energy: *Impetuousness. Rage. Giving up too quickly.*

Mantra: *I am here, I am now, fully present as I am.*

Let's begin!

And so we begin the journey, we are making a start. What's it like for you to start something new? Do you find yourself filled with energy, excitement and anticipation? Do you jump in enthusiastically, or do you approach new things more cautiously? We are setting out on a great adventure of the soul, initiating a process that will affect the way you see yourself, and it may prompt you to make certain changes in your life. We are about to turn the key in the ignition and fire up the engine. Notice how you feel as we enter the first gateway in the wheel, and ask yourself: *What is my intention here?*

Leaping into action

The wheel of the Zodiac is kicked off by Aries the ram, the fire sign with cardinal, initiatory motivation. Let us imagine him leaping into action, head first, with total conviction and fully committed to the passion of the moment. How often do you feel that in your life? Think of a time when you just went for it, when you wore your courage on your sleeve, and to hell with the consequences. When was the last time you seized the moment with full intention and acted, even if you didn't really know what you were doing or how it would turn out? Well, that's Aries in a nutshell; once we are committed to a course of action it takes that kind of energy to initiate it. If this doesn't sound like you, think of someone who fits this picture and remember a time when you were inspired by a courageous action of theirs. If you have an Aries Sun and you don't recognise this capacity, pay extra attention here because, latent within you, you most definitely carry this power of intention and initiation. We all possess it, but some of us are just more confident at expressing it when it's needed.

The passion of spring

Aries is the expression of spring in all its vibrant aliveness. The passage of the Sun through this sign in the northern hemisphere is a time when light conquers dark, beginning a period of six months when daylight prevails in length over night. With the increase of light comes the impulse for growth and Aries fully embodies the energy of new life awakening. New shoots make their presence felt as they break through the soil and each of us is prompted to awaken to what is new, vital and alive within ourselves, to find some manner of expressing that in the world. In the Aries phase we feel the urge, the irrepressible life force of the new bud breaking open on the branch or the birth of a child, and all the potential that such an event carries.

Only when imagination is alight with passion, enthused with desire, aflame with the inspiration of the moment, can one know that the journey has begun. This is the first scream of the newborn, the irrepressible enthusiasm of youth, the war-cry of the warrior's charge, the spiritual awakening that ignites our

hearts. To be 'enthused' is to be filled with God (*enthe deos*). To experience 'desire' is to be filled with the realisation that we have become separate from the stars (from *desiderata*).[1] The passion is fuelled by the intense suffering for what was once lost. To begin the quest for reunion and reconnection, we must burn with a longing to return. This is the Aries way.

The golden ram

Sometimes even the gods must seize the moment. When they do, the course of human history invariably takes a turn. Sometimes human beings are so stubborn and focused in their convictions that they completely fail to notice what is going on around them. And so it unfolded, one fateful day upon a great mountain in Boeotia, as a proud, wilful and impulsive father held a sacrificial flint to the throat of his beloved son. He had become convinced that the death of this son was a necessary appeasement to a god in order to restore the fertility of the land. Although we could be talking about the more familiar story of Abraham and Isaac, it is to an earlier variant of this archetypal narrative from which we draw our first mythic breath. On this turn of the wheel, the 'loudly weeping' father is Athamas and it is his son Phrixus whose life hangs by a thread, even as his face shines with the bright optimism of a new dawn.

The god in question, Zeus, had no interest in this human sacrifice, but it took a swift messenger to convey the news in time and a winged golden ram, sent by Hermes at Zeus's behest, swooped down to save him. His sister, Helle, also climbed aboard, her round face shimmering like the Moon. It is the Sun who is exalted in this story, however, and Helle did not survive the journey. The ram flew eastwards, delivering the child safely to the island of Colchis. Phrixus duly sacrificed the ram to Zeus, nailing its golden fleece to an oak tree in the sacred grove of Ares. A generation later, the great Arien warrior Jason and his assembly of Argonauts would famously arrive to claim it.[2]

To be born again

The journey eastward in this story is important; it points us in the direction of the dawn and of the Vernal or Spring Equinox, which marks the ascendancy of light over dark, day over night, Sun over Moon. The ram serves as an agent of resurrection and offers the possibility of new life, and the situation is taken to the brink before liberation comes. The story of Christ's crucifixion is also tied to the Spring Equinox, with Easter Sunday always set in the Christian calendar as the first Sunday after the first full moon after the Spring Equinox, carrying the theme of the resurrected son. Christ is frequently referred to as the Lamb of God because he was the perfect sacrifice, an obvious Arien reference.

New life springs forth

The Spring Equinox is one of the four major turning points of the solar year, and it marked the new year in Babylonian,

Greek, Roman and Persian calendars. Aries has huge importance as its stars are assumed to have been rising when the
world was being reconstructed after the Great Flood. The
temple of the ram-headed Amun-Ra at Karnak, in Egypt, was
oriented to the first degree of Aries at the vernal equinox in
1300 BCE.[3] The Spring Equinox carries a theme of liberation,
of new life following a period of hibernation, suffering,
retreat, fasting or loss. Its religious rites focus on a mythical
death and rebirth, as witnessed in Christianity and the cults
of solar/vegetation gods such as the Mesopotamian Tammuz
and later Marduk. In the Jewish tradition this is the time of
the Passover,[4] celebrated as the full moon rose over the eastern
horizon fourteen days into the first month of the year and
traditionally marked by the new moon in Aries. In later
Christianity, the key historical events of the Exodus of the
Israelites and the Crucifixion/Resurrection of Christ are
directly associated with this mytho-seasonal rebirth.[5]

Mars the warrior

The ruling planet of Aries is Mars. Unlike his Greek counterpart, Ares, he becomes highly dignified in the Roman world.
Both were gods of war, but Ares really had no other function
than this. He was seen as bloodthirsty, brutal, dangerous and
unforgiving, unlike the more favoured war goddess Athene,
who instilled her martial campaigns with wisdom and strategy.
The Roman Mars was first a god of agriculture, associated
with the energy of spring, the sowing of the seed and the

protection of the crop. As the Roman Empire spread, war and agriculture became more closely linked than one might imagine. Most Romans who fought in the early legions were farmers who had set aside their ploughs and scythes to pick up weapons when called upon to defend their lands. One thing that characterises strong Arien/Mars-type individuals is the way they fiercely protect their boundaries. Mars instils courage and the power to act, a force of will that, when well trained and focused on its goal, can be incisive and clinically effective. It's good to make some kind of commitment to Mars at this first stage of the wheel, for he brings vitality, virility and initiating presence.

Meeting life head-on

We could also call upon Athene, the wiser, more balanced Greek war goddess, born from the head of Zeus and representative of Aries among the twelve Olympian deities. Athene is a great strategist and it is essential to have her on your side if you go into battle, or any competitive situation, and want to win. Each sign of the zodiac rules a different part of the body and Athene's association with Aries is indicative of the fact that this sign rules the head. This should put us in mind of that moment when the force of nature drew us head first out of our mother's womb. Not all of us are born head first, of course, and the circumstances of our birth may have a bearing on our ability to meet life head-on.

Me first: the Aries shadow energy

There is a wonderful film, *The Gods Must be Crazy*, which follows the lives of a small, resourceful tribe living in peace, harmony and cooperation in the Kalahari Desert. One day a plane flies overhead and the pilot mindlessly throws an empty Coke bottle out of the window. It lands in the small settlement and is initially seen by the tribe as a gift from the gods. Having never seen such a thing before, it immediately becomes a source of great wonder, and is able to be put to many and varied uses. But because there is only one, it soon creates competition and conflict among the tribe, as the younger members fight over it and selfishly covet it. Anger, jealousy and hate, previously unknown emotions, arise within the community, causing great concern among the elders, and a feeling of shame comes over the members of the suddenly divided group. This poignant tale points to the Aries shadow, which is that self-serving, me-first, aggressive impulse that we each carry, which is borne of the blind, naïve and ultimately shaming conviction that there is only one way, one truth, one winner, one of me against all of you.

The shadow of too much Aries

When you have an excess of Aries medicine your energy tends to get powerfully unleashed in the passion of the moment. If it is not grounded in some concrete intention, project or activity, your soul can be like tinder, liable to set alight at any moment. This is the first place in the wheel where we can get stuck, as passion turns into anger and destructive rage. Often this is born of frustration that the world around you is failing to meet your demand for everything to happen now. It manifests as impatience and intolerance, which can alienate others. It might cause you to give up too easily on a new venture when things don't immediately go your way. If this is true for you, learn to take an extra breath before acting, allow in experiences that bring you more in touch with your senses, your body, give yourself more time for contemplation, to appreciate the beauty around you. Look to the medicine of the opposite sign, Libra, for balance and consideration.

The shadow of not enough Aries

Having a lack of Mars/Aries energy can be just as damaging to your well-being. Characterised by a lack of drive or a lack of will, you would more likely hesitate when action is called for, fail to respond in the moment when an opportunity arises and look to others to be your driving force. In this case, your anger tends to be displaced and you may find that your passivity draws out another's frustration, particularly if that other carries an excess of the Mars medicine. If Mars is weak in your birthchart, this can make it more difficult for you to align with your intention and find the motivation to get things started. If so, let this medicine inspire you. Connect with Mars's metal, iron; maybe pump some down at the gym, and check that you have enough of this mineral in your diet. Take in warming foods and energy-boosting tonics. Practise channelling your energy in more direct, assertive and decisive ways. It's not that you lack fire; you just haven't brought enough attention to this capacity within you. Now is the time to do that.

Take a moment to read this poem by Dorsha Hayes.

Fire Hazard

Filled with the clutter of unsorted stuff
A spark can set a man ablaze
What's there heaped high among stored rubbish,
At a puff will burst into flame.
No man can be aware of how inflammable he is,
How prone to what can rage beyond control,
Unless the piled up litter of his life
Is known to him, and he is able to assess
What hazard he is in, what could ignite.
A man disordered and undisciplined
Lives in the peril of a panic flight
Before the onrush of a flaming wind.
Does it now seem I seek to be profound?
I stand on smoking ash and blackened ground.[6]

I recommend reading this poem each day that you spend on the Aries stage of the journey; keep returning to it throughout the whole process. It carries an alchemical key that speaks to the urgency within each of us to finally say 'enough is enough' and commit to awakening to the power of our initiative for the good of ourselves and for the good of all. You don't need to interpret the poem beyond that. Just let it work on you.

Kairos: the right moment to act

Aries puts us in the heat of moment, and instils in us an urgency to begin. The Greek word *kairos*, unlike the more familiar, measurable concept of time, *chronos*, describes a non-linear, qualitative experience of the moment, a 'time out of time': boundless, eternal, a moment of full and uncompromising presence. This is also the propitious time, 'the right moment', for action, a moment loaded with serendipity and meaningful correspondence. I have always been inspired by this and have placed the idea at the very heart of all my astrological work, even naming my business Kairos Astrology. I experienced a wonderful serendipity just a year after I did this, when I found myself in Croatia in a town called Trogir, which was founded by Greek colonists in the third century BCE. There was a revelation in store for me there. I had always assumed up to that point that *kairos* was simply a concept in Greek thought. (I should have known better, as ancient people quite naturally deify and animate all their conceptual ideas.) In Trogir I stumbled upon a rare bas-relief of Kairos, the 'God of the Fleeting Moment': a young man, winged and running, with a prominent tuft of hair for a fringe and bald at the back.[7] When Kairos enters your life, you have to grab him by his tuft of hair. If you wait a moment too long, he will get away from you, and there is nothing at his back to grab hold of! *Carpe diem*. As Aries poet William Wordsworth succinctly put it: 'To begin, begin'.

Cracking open the alchemical egg

In the Pelasgian creation myth we find a supreme goddess figure called Eurynome, who dances upon the waves of Ocean. She is fertilised by the serpent Ophion, whom she has created through her dancing. Transforming herself into a dove, she lays an egg upon the waters, around which Ophion entwines himself until such time as the egg cracks and the world issues forth. Ophion and Eurynome then take their place on Mount Olympus, where they rule together until Ophion begins to brag about how he had actually made the world himself, with no help from anyone. The response of the goddess is direct and unforgiving. She kicks out his teeth and banishes him to the Underworld. From these teeth springs Pelasgus, who comes to teach man all of the arts and crafts.[8]

An alchemical exercise for contemplation

The hatching of an egg is the perfect Arien symbol. There is a reason why eggs are the symbol of Easter, which draws much of its symbolism from the pagan Oestre. There is a seventeenth-century alchemical image from Michael Maier's *Atlanta Fugiens* of a male figure standing over an egg, with a furnace burning fiercely in the hearth alongside the room in which he stands. From the attached engraving, we can assume that this is the philosophical egg of alchemy and that the figure is Vulcan, the Smith God.[9]

We encourage students on The Alchemical Journey to study the image, which can be sourced online, with this question in mind: 'When will he strike?' There is caution in his approach and a great deal of focus, his eyes passionately trained on the egg. In order for the new life inside to be born vital, it must bring through the energy generated in the heat of the Smith God's intention. If the man strikes prematurely, he will kill the mother essence that lies at the heart of the egg and the chick will die. However, if he loses presence, hesitates, waits too long for fear of doing harm, the chick will lack the energy to break the shell and will die *in utero*. He must align his masculine will with the feminine power of the creation force, and strike precisely at the moment when the egg is ready to crack open under its own natural means. This is the *kairos* moment.

Let us heed the warning in Ophion's fall from grace and remain ever mindful of the origins of life. Man is born of woman and while his seed must remain vital in order to maintain the cycle of life, he never acts alone; he is wholly interdependent with the feminine as the source of creative power, and as the vessel through which new life emerges.

Aries summary

The following exercises can help you contemplate your relationship to the Aries energy and find your own unique way into it. This is a process of action and reflection. Work with your journal and do something concrete that shows your commitment to make a start. Pay particular attention this month to moments of inspiration, passion, creative spark, vision, excitement, anger, courage, sexual arousal or anything else that awakens a fiery impulse in you!

CONSIDER THESE QUESTIONS, ASK YOURSELF:

- What are you really passionate about, what's burning inside you?

- What rejuvenates you, makes you feel most alive?

- What is your intention for your journey ahead?

- What could you actively do now to commit to that intention?

- What are you willing to risk in service of this quest?

SUGGESTED ACTIVITIES

- Find three people who know you well. Be bold; ask them these questions, notice your response:
  * What was your first impression of me when we first met?
  * What particular qualities do I possess that make me stand out as who I am?
  * What do you think holds me back from manifesting all the things I want in my life?

- Think of something that you've wanted to do for a long time, but have been putting off. Before moving on to the next sign, either do it, or make a definite step towards making it happen.

- Take a flower seed and plant it in a pot. As you do, infuse it with your intention. Write it down and plant it in the soil. Speak it out. Then in the following days and weeks, pay daily attention to it. Spend time with it, water it, speak to it. Develop a relationship with what you have planted. Notice what happens as you do, and notice when you forget or neglect it. What happens to the seed – whether it sprouts successfully, whether it flowers or not, whether it grows tall or short – is less important that the ritual of just paying attention to your own process of committing to your intention.

- Spend some time with an Aries friend or someone with strong Mars energy. Let yourself be inspired by their enthusiasm and will for action.

The Second Gateway

Taurus

Sun in Taurus period: *19/20 April – 20/21 May*

Symbol: *The Bull*

Motivation: *Fixed/establishing and maintaining*

Element (temperament): *Earth*

Ruling planet: *Venus*

Body parts ruled: *Throat and neck*

Keynote: *Here it is, I want to have it. Now I've got it, I want to keep it.*

Version of the truth: *The garden is growing.*

Medicine: *Gratitude. What you appreciate, appreciates.*

Shadow energy: *Greed. Possessiveness. Complacency. Holding on to stuff.*

Mantra: *I am fully embodied here in the sensuality of this moment.*

The transition from Aries to Taurus

The second sign of the zodiac is Taurus, the earth sign with fixed motivation that consolidates and grounds the creative impulse in material reality. After all the creative energy, fiery force and head-first enthusiasm of Aries, in our second zodiac medicine we encounter a perfect counterbalance: a slow-moving, sensuous, embodied sign, looking to satisfy herself with the good things in life. Mars the warrior must now give way to Venus the lover. The cusps between the signs, where we transition from one to the next, are places of tension, vulner-ability and fertility. Every zodiac sign has two neighbouring signs that possess very different natures to its own; they do not simply merge into one another and the transition is not supposed to be smooth. Making the shift to the next sign is akin to an initiation. Each transition requires that we let go of any attachments we have to the previous perspective as we enter the very different world of what follows. If we have fully embraced and incorporated the lessons of each phase an integration occurs at this point and the transition is more natural. Notice where you are as we move into Taurus now.

Irresistible force meets immovable object!

Whenever I consider the Aries-Taurus transition, the 'irresist-ible force' paradox comes to mind. All that creative firepower – wild, free, everywhere and in every moment – is now met by a powerful and overwhelming desire for embodiment. That incredible energy of creation is compelled by gravity to land somewhere, in something tangible that can be fully experienced through the five senses. This is where the creative impulse for life becomes flesh. If we are totally immersed in the full-blown enthusiasm of Aries, the conditions that this earthy desire imposes on us can feel abrupt and restrictive, to say the least. It's the moment when you think you've come up with the most brilliant invention of all time, which will probably change the world as we know it, and are met with the response: 'Come on, get real!', or, more likely, 'I'm hungry, let's eat.' It's a come-down, a reality check; it brings us down to earth with a bump. It addresses the matter to which the Arien passion and drive must now apply itself and the focus of attention is the belly!

Grounding the inspiration

Can you identify a time in your life when your enthusiasm for a new idea or project waned because you couldn't see any concrete proof of it working in reality? In this second stage of the wheel we are more likely to assess whether something is real or not through the evidence of our five senses, or else we judge its validity by whether or not it offers us material security. In Aries, we had faith in our creative vision, but now we need to feel the value of it in our bodies, or see its effects in our bank accounts. Can you recognise that conflict within you? Have you ever given up too quickly on an inspirational idea because it didn't bear fruit immediately, and ended up settling for the safer bet? Or perhaps you keep faith with your initiatives but fail to 'land' them in a way that sustains your well-being. Notice if you tend more towards creative idealism or practical realism. If you can identify an imbalance here, it might be to do with your sense of self-worth and your ability to appreciate the rich array of resources that you have available to you. Hold these questions in mind as we enter the Taurean gateway.

The sacred cow of abundance

Taurus is one of the most impressive constellations in the night sky, one loaded with mythic significance. This bovine stellar effigy preserves the memory of a more than two-thousand-year-old astrological age (circa 4000–1500 BCE) that included the great bull-oriented Minoan civilisation, founded after Europa was carried off by Zeus in the form of a white bull, from Asia to Crete. Europa is commonly depicted tying a garland of spring flowers to the bull's horns, or around his lusty neck. Despite this image of a testosterone-laden bull, however, the energy of Taurus is primarily feminine. She is Hathor, the Egyptian cow-goddess whose milk feeds a young pharaoh and nurtures his divine destiny. It is her milk that splashes across the sky in the river of stars we know as the Milky Way. In early Greek myth, we find Zeus's wife Hera represented as a white moon-cow, symbolising her abundant love and nourishing gift of sustenance. These stories speak of a life-sustaining power that feeds growth and brings prosperity.

Taurus is the sign of exaltation for the Moon, who reveals her 'cow horns' during her waxing crescent phase in Egyptian and southern Mediterranean latitudes.

The season of sensuous abundance

The mighty bull or sacred cow of heaven takes centre stage in our astrological imaginations as the Sun enters Taurus in the third week of April, a time when the Aries buds, bursting with potential, sprout their beautiful, sweet-smelling blossoms. The generous abundance of spring reveals itself, presents the most bounteous gifts to the senses, offering us an enticing preview of the summer harvest to come, as days lengthen and daylight establishes its dominance over darkness. There is growth in nature; a sense of prosperity feeds our growing appetite, and there is much feasting. We sense that the good life is there for us to enjoy, and we are led by our bellies!

During this period of the year, the pagan festival of Beltane marks the beginning of May, a celebration of fertility and abundance. It is the birth of summer in the Celtic calendar, when the Green Man, or Jack-o-the-Green, reclaims his power from Jack Stag, the Winter King, and in a great fertility rite he marries the May Queen. The 'bringing in of the may', the collecting of hawthorn blossoms, is a traditional activity associated with this time of the year and a theme around which many a merry folk tune has been sung.[1] The dance around the strong, erect maypole, which is placed in a hole dug into the feminine earth, honours the heightened sexual energy that is alive in nature at this time of year. The May Day dancers tie red and white ribbons around the pole as they circle it, creating a weave of masculine and feminine energy, red for the female menstrual blood and white for the male semen.[2]

So Taurus is charged with both sensuous and sexual energy. Mars and Venus have united at the cusp of Aries and Taurus, and an erotic coupling has taken place. Venus (Greek Aphrodite), the goddess of love and beauty, is the ruling planet of this sign and carries a powerful magnetism that is irresistibly attractive, brimming with fertility. Allowing herself to be impregnated by Mars's potent seed, she becomes radiantly alive, rosy-cheeked and fully embodied in her feminine essence. The third Tarot trump, the Empress, perfectly illustrates this through a figure that seems completely content, surrounded by the sensuous bounty of her garden, which blesses and honours her.[3]

How much have I got and is it enough?

Our enquiry now shifts from the fiery immediacy of *What's burning in me?* and *How do I begin?* to more earthy, grounded questions, such as: *What do I have?*, *What am I worth?* and *How do I secure my lot?* In this stage of the journey we take account of ourselves and begin to evaluate our resources.

How much have I got, and is it enough? should provoke a deep enquiry for you. How much is enough? So many of us have been conditioned from an early age to believe that there is never enough, and we have bought into a philosophy of life founded upon lack. We are told very early on that there is only so much to go around, that we need to hold on to what we have. This belief in lack easily spreads to encompass all aspects of life, and we start believing that there is not enough time, not enough space, not enough love; this can do great damage to our sense of self-worth. Does this sound familiar? In truth, though, if we look around at nature we can see that this 'toxic myth of scarcity' (as global activist Lynne Twist has called it) is a lie.⁴ And the sign of Taurus, the sign of abundance, offers us the perfect opportunity to realise this as she blossoms with nature's gift. There is enough to go around if we can but see how nature provides us with all that we need.

But this belief in 'not enough' fuels a second, perhaps more damaging, conviction that *more is better*, which then drives a competitive mindset of accumulation, acquisition and greed, none of which actually makes life more valuable.

> ... greed and fear of scarcity are programmed; they do not exist in nature, not even in human nature. They are built into the money system in which we swim, and we've been swimming in it so long that these shadows have become almost completely transparent to us.⁵

Terrible twos!

One way of understanding this is to consider that the urge for acquisition is rooted in our very earliest experiences as children. At this point in the human life cycle we have moved beyond the newborn phase of Aries, where there is no concept of a distinction between ourselves and the rest of the world; now we are at the age of perhaps two years and we are definitely aware of things that are *not me*. So arises the urge to acquire them and secure them: *if they are not me, then I must make them mine*. This is the so-called 'terrible twos', where the child learns the words 'no' and 'it's mine', and with it the impulse to grab and keep hold of things. The urge to own, acquire and hold on to what we have develops early and the righteous pursuit of individual acquisition is a dominant myth of our times, which is why so many of us get stuck here. Ask yourself: *How able am I to simply trust that everything I need is provided for me?*

The Taurus shadow: the myth of the Minotaur

King Minos of Crete, son of Zeus and Europa, summoned a sacred white bull out of the sea, promising to sacrifice it to Poseidon one year hence. That year the kingdom flourished; the land was especially fertile and great prosperity was enjoyed by all. Times were so prosperous, however, and the royal house so lauded with praise, that Minos decided the bull was too precious to sacrifice and so he kept it, breaking his promise to the god of the sea. Going against the will of the gods like this doesn't usually turn out well, and Poseidon placed a curse on Minos's queen, Pasiphae, who was driven wild with lust for the sacred animal. She employed the master craftsman Daedalus to build a wooden cow within which she might conceal herself, so that the bull might be inclined to mate with her. Unlikely as this might sound, the unnatural act did indeed occur, and resulted in the birth of Asterius, better known as the Minotaur: a half-man, half-bull creature with an insatiable appetite for human flesh. Daedalus was again summoned, this time to build the mighty labyrinth that would house the creature and keep him from destroying the kingdom. This was duly done, but his appetite continued to rage and could only be satisfied with the flesh of young men, who were shipped in on a regular basis from the Greek mainland. One such youth, Theseus, was to finally overcome the Minotaur with the help of Minos's daughter, Ariadne, who provided him with the golden thread, enabling him to find his way out of the labyrinth once he had slain her bull-headed half-brother.[6]

As for the white bull, following his night of passion with the queen, he turned wild himself and could not be controlled. It took Hercules to catch him – one of his twelve labours – and take him away to the mainland, where he escaped and roamed about the Peloponnese until Theseus, by now somewhat expert in dealing with wild bulls, captured him at Marathon and offered the bull to his father, who duly sacrificed it to Apollo.[7]

In the grip of the bull

The story speaks for itself and hardly needs interpretation. What is more important is that you find your place in the story, some aspect of it with which you can identify, even if it is uncomfortable. If so, allow its medicine to work on you. What compels us from a zodiac perspective is the way that these stories about fertility, prosperity, acquisition, gain and its shadow of greed are so often associated with the bull. In the world of finance and investment, the term 'bull market' is used to describe a period of growth and optimism where stocks of securities are rising, or expected to rise, in price. On Wall Street in New York City there is a large bronze statue of a charging bull, surely put there to reflect or even invoke the energy and strength of a stock market whose demand for growth at any cost is as insatiable and lustful as the characters in our story. The bull is a stubborn character; it holds on to what it desires and it can really get a grip on us. Notice where it has its grip on you.

True wealth and the soul of money

Taurus takes its fill like no other sign other of the zodiac, brimming with satiety like a laughing Buddha, reminding us to appreciate nature's gifts and to savour the sensuous pleasures of life that are gifted to us, yet without getting attached to them. This fat Buddha figure, the so-called Buddha of Abundance, is not smiling with satisfaction for all that he has;

he is laughing outrageously at the paradox of life, which gives with one hand and takes away with the other.[8] The wisdom in the Buddha's laughter points to the deeper lesson of Taurus: enjoy what we have, *while we have it.*

This might make us reconsider what we mean by wealth. The word actually comes from the old English word 'weal', meaning well-being, and is pronounced the same as 'wheel'. So I consider myself to be truly wealthy when I allow the turning wheel of well-being to bless me. From such a perspective, wealth really has nothing to do with the accumulation of money. It is a dynamic – not a static – condition of being; a living art, a capacity that we all have to attract an abundant flow of energy, monetary or otherwise. A truly wealthy person hasn't sold their soul or sacrificed their time for money. They live life by being authentically themselves and naturally attracting happiness, health, love and sufficient financial resources to enable their wheel to turn, to be able to respond to life's changing circumstances without the anxiety of lack or the fear of loss. What is money, after all, if not an energy that flows through our lives, a medium of exchange keeping us in a dynamic relationship with the world around us? Lynne Twist describes money 'as a current, a carrier, a conduit for our intentions'.[9] She goes so far as to say that it carries the imprint of our soul, revealing how far we have come from such an understanding, and how we have come to both idolise and demonise something which is ultimately benign, apart from our excessive coveting of it. In Aries we set our intention and it gave us a direction. Now, through Taurus, that intention can become embodied and find its carrier. We must address our relationship with money for this embodiment to be authentic. It brings up big issues, not least because of the level of inequity and corruption within our monetary systems. If we can allow it, though, this money energy can flow through our lives and bring a genuine sense of prosperity.

Re-establishing a sense of self-worth

> To find the soul of modern man and woman, begin
> by searching into those irreducibly embarrassing
> facts of the money complex, the crazy crab
> scuttling across the floors of silent seas.[10]

Money resonates with some deep part of us, and modern money systems (based almost exclusively on speculation and debt) that we are forced to operate within undoubtedly shape the fears and emotions that we all experience. Our distorted economies have much to do with the imbalances we feel in our lives. So it follows that, as we start to consider the deep-seated beliefs we have around money, we open up a parallel enquiry around self-worth. That question: *Is there enough?* very easily slips into the unsettling psychological anxiety: *Am I enough?* So often our striving for more is not just an attempt to secure our financial security but is rather more deeply motivated towards proving our self-worth. However, when the structure of our life is founded on the belief that there isn't enough, no matter how much we attain or achieve, it will never satisfy us. Thus the work at this stage requires us to examine that fundamental, underlying, lack-centred thought pattern, a pattern that is exploited and reinforced by the nature of capitalist culture and the inequity of modern money systems. We must reintegrate a deep appreciation of nature's cycles into our lives, both around money and our evaluation of self.

Contemplate the abundance that flows through you naturally, the things that are always, already there, which require no striving from you. Taurus presents us with our 'God-given' resources and talents, our natural abilities that arise spontaneously from our embodiment in the world, and we can recognise them as our personal resources. In this early phase of the wheel, take some time to assess and appreciate what talents you have available to you and nurture and appreciate those qualities. The sense of lack that we feel is largely a problem of perception. Let the living, breathing animal of your body reassure you; there is enough, you have enough, you are enough. There is a medicine readily available to us to address the perceptual anomaly that seems to convince us otherwise, and that is the medicine of gratitude.

The Taurus medicine: gratitude

Think of a Taurean person you know, or someone who embodies those qualities: someone really grounded, really connected to nature, someone who feels like they could have been grown out of the earth. Remember what it was like being with them; perhaps you took a walk with them around their lush, abundant garden; maybe you stopped to smell the flowers; maybe you enjoyed a meal with them and really let yourself savour the food and the company. Do you remember how all your worries and concerns seemed less important than they had been before? This is the effect of good Taurus medicine: being grateful for what's right in front of you, recognising its beauty, letting it fill up your senses and satisfy you right there, in that moment. So often our attention is elsewhere, either in another place or time, past or future. Taurus medicine brings us into the present moment through the wondrous sensorium of our human bodies. Gratitude is a practice that is good for everyone; it is a key component of most religious systems and a vital component of the manifest-ation process. When you are grateful for what you have and express that gratitude in some active way each day, your perception of what you have or your relationship with it begins to change; you find yourself attracting more things to be grateful for. Begin this daily practice during this phase of the journey and it will serve as a vital tool for getting your wheel turning again.

Taurus summary

These questions and exercises are designed to help you nourish and nurture your relationship with the medicine of Taurus. The questions for enquiry are designed to stimulate response and reflection. Continue working with your journal and note down any insights and inspirations that arise.

CONSIDER THESE QUESTIONS, ASK YOURSELF:

- What are my anxieties and fears around money?

- In which areas of my life do I experience a sense of lack?

- What do I have to be grateful for?

- How much is enough for me?

SUGGESTED EXERCISES AND ACTIVITIES

- Begin a daily practice of gratitude. Spend fifteen minutes every day either writing down or saying aloud things about your life for which you are grateful.

- Spend time in nature, in the garden. Smell the flowers, get your hands in the soil, feel the good earth, open your senses.

- Be mindful around cooking and the food that you eat. Eat slowly; chew your food more thoroughly. Stay present with the food as you swallow it, before taking another mouthful.

- Become more aware of your body. Treat yourself to a full body massage. Experience and become more aware of the sensation of touch; notice the effects of this.

- Spend some time taking account of the money in your life. Get your bank statements in order, notice how much you have, how much you spend, what you spend it on. Become more aware of the flow of money in and out of your life.

- Recall a successful endeavour. Note what talents of yours were brought to bear upon that task. Imagine ways in which these special talents might be employed in other areas of your life.

The Third Gateway

Gemini

Sun in Gemini period: *20/21 May – 20/21 June*

Symbol: *The Twins*

Motivation: *Mutable/adapting and transforming*

Element (temperament): *Air*

Ruling planet: *Mercury*

Body parts ruled: *Arms, hands, shoulders, lungs*

Keynote: *I'm listening, I want to hear. Keep talking, I want to know.*

Version of the truth: *There are different versions of the truth.*

Medicine: *Articulation. Using language to create reality.*

Shadow energy: *Loose talk. Gossip. Inconsistency.*

Mantra: *I am a messenger of light, a conduit for the voice of my spirit twin to be heard.*

The transition from Taurus to Gemini

There is a wind getting up now, disturbing the peace and tranquillity of the garden, blowing the blossoms from the trees. It is a wind of change; it is blowing through our minds, just when we thought we were getting settled. It can be an uncomfortable transition and this mutable air sign can feel destabilising, make us uncertain. In many ways our security is at risk, everything is in flux, things flapping about; it is hard to keep track of what belongs to whom. We hear the capricious wind whispering something in our ear and we cannot ignore it. It promises knowledge, pathways of understanding, new information that enables us to see everything around us in a new light, and however much it threatens the status quo, it is utterly irresistible.

Lightening the load

The urge in the Taurus phase of the wheel is to establish the value of what we have, to stake our claim for the things that make us feel secure and give us pleasure, and to acquire the deeds to them. Establishing ownership is a necessary stage of both personal and community development. It gives substance to our creative impulses and ensures that we become responsible guardians. But our guardianship is only temporary; we will all die one day. In certain cultures, if you were to especially admire a particular artefact that belonged to someone else, that person would then be obliged to give it to you.[1] How would you feel about that? Think about how much of yourself you have invested in the things that you own. How much time and energy do you devote to securing them against loss? Or are you someone who is more likely to let things slip through their fingers? Do you prefer to avoid the responsibilities of owner-ship wherever possible? The Geminian perspective invites us to become more flexible in our relationship to the things we acquire in our lives. It inspires in us the inventiveness to trade, exchange, borrow, lend and steal. And perhaps more profoundly, it awakens in us the ingenuity to substitute the value we place in tangible stuff for the value of words, symbols and ideas. In order to progress, we need to make ourselves as light as possible. Of course, it is not really the things that we own that weigh us down, but our attachment to them. Consider this then, as you enter through the Gemini portal now: *Is there anything you could meaningfully leave at the gate?*

The Twins

This sign is symbolised by twin brothers who share a common origin, born together yet seeded from different fathers, one human and one divine. They are thus distinctly polarised in nature, the mortal Castor and the immortal Pollux. Known as the Dioscuri, the inseparable pair are always shown riding together in tandem. The mortal Castor is killed during a cattle raid (a Gemini theme), and Pollux begs Zeus to let him die so that the two can be reunited. Zeus refuses, but he does allow the immortal twin to grant half of his divinity to his mortal brother; thus they can live half their time in the Underworld and half on Mount Olympus, alternating between light and dark, allowed to participate in both worlds. The twins offer humankind both light and shadow; they became patrons of travellers, rescuers in times of need, able to survive the descent into the dark, the journey of night, of death, and the return to the light. They share this privilege with the messenger Hermes, the Roman Mercury (another cattle thief), the ruling planetary deity of Gemini. More on him later ...

The sign of duality

Gemini is the first sign of duality that we meet in the wheel. Both Aries and Taurus carry an instinctive, single-minded conviction. Now, the truth is betwixt and between. With Gemini comes dialogue and interaction; the twins are rapt in a perpetual conversation, an ongoing exchange of information that keeps them forever connected, yet forever dual. The Gemini glyph looks very similar to its own star constellation, shown as two pillars connected by a bar above and below. I choose to see it as a temple doorway, a portal into a hall of learning where words and ideas carry an efficacious power. Once we step across this threshold we are changed and must confront the duality within our own nature. This stage of the wheel is a meditation on the way we think and put ideas together, the things we believe, the way we speak, the way we respond to different stimuli and, ultimately, the way we create our reality through what we think and the language that we use.

The buzz

The Sun sign period of Gemini begins around 21 May each year and takes us up to the Summer Solstice, the longest day of the year. Daylight continues to increase in the northern hemisphere, with the Sun rising higher in the sky towards its seasonal zenith. The chattering twins invite us into the mysteries of the air element and Mother Nature responds with a rich variety of sounds, colours, scents and textures. The blossoms of Taurus have attracted bees to every flower; the Geminian messengers buzz around happily from one source of interest to another, transferring information. Everything seems up for grabs in this hubbub of trade and exchange.

In the Christian calendar this seasonal transformation is perfectly echoed in the festival of Pentecost, or Whitsuntide. Traditionally the fiftieth day after Easter, it will usually occur while the Sun is in Gemini, when the Holy Spirit descends from heaven and visits upon the disciples of Christ. It comes as a rushing wind, carrying wit and knowledge, inspiring the apostles to spread the 'good news' of the Christian message far and wide, like pollinating bees. This is often considered to be the birth of the Church. The apostles are said to have suddenly

found themselves speaking in foreign languages – speaking in
tongues. People passing by first thought that they must be
drunk, with all their babbling, but the apostle Peter told the
crowd that his fellow apostles were full not of liquor but of
the Holy Spirit.[2]

The emissaries of the air

Spiritual traditions the world over conceive the air as being full
of intermediary beings: spirits, angels, daemons, siddhe,
fairies, jinn and so on; mediators between human beings and
their gods. In our modern world, we are generally disenchanted
of such ideas. Nowadays the air is filled not with spirit beings
but with our mobile phone and Wi-Fi signals transmitting our
constant human jabberings and data exchanges; spiritually
diminished but still thoroughly Geminian. For our pre-modern
ancestors, and for indigenous groups still operating today, the
primary application of language was, and is, to engage in
dialogue with these animating powers of the inbetween realm.
They would make some form of ritual appeal to divine what
best course of action should be taken, then look for signs of
response, perhaps through observing anomalies, for example,
in the flight patterns of birds.

Jung said the gods have become the psychological archetypes. Similarly the daemons, the emissaries of the air, have
been divested of their sensuous, divinatory power, and are now
bound up as concepts within linguistic structures. But they
haven't disappeared, they have gone underground, where they

lurk menacingly in the hidden corners of the psyche. As Patrick Harpur puts it:

> Nowadays we do not heed the daimons and so they reproach us from their current home, the unconscious, with unruly behaviour that we try to quieten with secular rituals, such as stress management, psychotherapy, drugs, fitness regimes, relaxation techniques, recreational games and so on, none of which imaginatively accommodates – that is, enshrines – the daimons at their proper distance from us, and their proper nearness.[3]

They can be released from those conceptual structures, at least temporarily, through the arts. Poets, artists, dancers, musicians (and modern-day diviners) all seek some level of discourse with daemons, and will make some form of creative attempt to unbind them.

So many questions!

Because of its dualistic nature, the Gemini stage of our soul wheel brings with it continual dilemmas as to how to think, how to behave, what to say, which direction to follow and how to respond to the ever-changing conditions of life. How should we interpret the signs that appear to us? If we don't believe in signs, how should we be guided, by what or by whom? This brings up ethical issues, an area traditionally managed by religion; but in an increasingly secular world, it is left more up to one's own individual conscience and moral code. Of the voices we hear, both from others and within our heads, which are true and which are false? Which choices will lead us towards our goals, what other agendas are at play? So many questions, so many potential pathways we could follow, it can be endlessly confusing. How do we choose?

Hermes, the trickster thief

One truly ingenious character stands apart from all other members of the Greek pantheon, and that is Hermes. He bestows the gifts of language, communication and commerce. He is patron of storytellers, thieves and magicians, of orators, travellers and traders. He is the duplicitous divine messenger: trickster, wordsmith, riddler, diviner and creator of culture. As Roman Mercury, he is named for the planet that moves fastest while never straying far from the Sun, flickering briefly each morning in the pre-dawn sky before disappearing into the Underworld, and reappearing a few weeks later in the fading light of evening. As a god he is forever young; as soon as he is born he hops from his cot and invents the lyre, ripping out the innards of a tortoise, using its shell as a sound chamber and its guts for strings. He plays it for a while, then tires of it and pursues his next vocation as thief, stealing the cattle from under the nose of his older brother, Apollo. With this first theft comes the first lie: *Who me, a mere child, stealing from mighty Apollo? You must be mistaken!* With the first lie comes the first act of creativity, the beginning of the art of language, as Hermes conjures up the first stirrings of human culture.[4]

The first symbolic act

The Gemini phase is that moment in childhood when we first learn to substitute words for things. With this comes the ability to use language to further our own interests. It takes us beyond the Taurean belly urge – 'it's mine' – and into the Geminian impulse for dialogue, interaction and exchange. When Hermes steals the cattle, his thieving impulse is initially motivated by hunger, but then he makes a uniquely original gesture, dividing the different parts of two of the animals and offering them to the gods, without partaking of the meat himself. It is sometimes considered by mythologists to be the first instance of sacrifice.[5] The meat is made sacred through a symbolic gesture designed to convince the gods to show leniency.

Language, too, originates as a gestural appeal and we use it in a similar way to help us get what we want. As children we learn to use language and gesture to manipulate the will of our parents. Those of us who learn to master this art early on tend to get away with it, appearing so cute, so adorable, that butter wouldn't melt! Like all of us, to a certain extent, Hermes is in an ambiguous position; he has been born into lowly circumstances yet seeks to be reunited with what he knows are his divine origins. He is the cleverest of the gods; in deferring his immediate appetite for the sake of a greater reward later on, he wins their favour. He has his divine status recognised and is uniquely permitted to cross the boundaries between worlds, passing information between gods and humans.

Stories make us human

With the invention of lying comes the ability to use language creatively; the capacity to imagine, describe and manipulate different perceptions of reality. This is the art of storytelling; it is the basis of culture, and what makes us essentially human. Stories are where we live, and we are all master storytellers. However much we might like to think we base our lives on concrete facts, our experience is conditioned by our interpretations of life's circumstances. Yet we forget this all the time! We forget that the story we tell about what happened when a relationship ended six years ago is merely an updated version of the last time we told that story. Our interpretations of reality change as our perceptions of ourselves change; we are continually fine-tuning our narratives. These tend to feature ourselves as 'the noble – if flawed – protagonists of first-person dramas', never an objective account, as every line of it is 'replete with strategic forgetting and skillfully spun meanings'.[6] No matter what happens to us, we will interpret it in such a way as to make it fit the account we want to be known. The way we perceive something will depend greatly upon our cultural context, our early childhood experiences, our upbringing, the type of education we received, and so on. If you lose your job, if someone steals from you, if you are falsely accused of something, a whole chain of interpretive moves will be set in motion in your mind, based on your past experiences and the patterns of belief associated with them. However, and this is the crucial aspect of Geminian medicine, we can always choose how we respond to any given situation; the more conscious awareness we can bring to each moment, the more freedom we will have to respond differently. Stories awaken the soul and can help us to see life from different perspectives. We all have the power to make up different stories to those we are used to.

Spell-ing

In Old English, 'to spell' meant to recite a story. Nowadays, we understand the word in two different ways: 'letters arranged in the correct order', on the one hand; 'a magical formula or charm', on the other.[7] They seem radically different, but are they really? We are so accustomed to using words in our everyday lives – thinking, speaking, emailing, tweeting – that we easily forget the power they have over us and others. Modern linguistic theories based around nominalism more or less reduce words to dead, quasi-mathematical units, probably because we have come to think of them as individual units 'spelled' out on the page. Yet we all know that in the hands of a skilled poet or orator those words can be reanimated with the power to enchant and awaken perception in ways that can directly alter our ways of seeing things. The ancient Greeks considered rhetoric – the skilful arrangement of words delivered in a powerful and compelling way – to be one of the highest arts. The politician employs this art to persuade his audience of the essential truth of a particular idea, the poet to illuminate an unseen dimension of reality, the mythologist to reawaken the sleeping, stillborn, dead parts of the psyche, the culture and the world.

Learning to see in two worlds

Hermes is granted the ability to travel freely between the upperworld and the Underworld. As the God of the Crossroads, anywhere a crossing can be made, Hermes will be present. It is said that every daemon, every intermediary being who dwells on the liminal borders between light and shade, between sleeping and waking, is a different face of Hermes.[8] Part of the art that we can develop at this stage of the turning wheel is the ability to see in two separate worlds, to develop what William Blake called 'double vision', where the eye of imagination can see through the physical manifestation to its spirit twin in the unseen realm.

Loose talk and gossip: the Gemini shadow energy

So how do you use words? How much time do you spend talking *about* what happens around you, talking about what you believe to be the case in any given situation? How much time do you spend bemoaning the state of your life, or complaining *about* the way other people act or behave? Let's face it: this 'loose talk and gossip' probably constitutes the majority of the words that issue from our mouths, as we give voice to thoughts whose repetitive patterns continuously rattle around in our minds. Words carry tremendous power and reinforce our existing beliefs about the way the world is, the way other people are, the choices we have available to us. Loose talk and gossip tends to become a self-fulfilling prophecy, reducing the scope of our imaginations, limiting our ability to see things differently, and convincing us that we are powerless to change our lives. We entangle ourselves in stories that inevitably fail to inspire us, and damaging self-talk based on limited perceptions of reality.

The air as a medium of sacred address

Now think about how different it is when we address the world directly, when we draw inspiration from what is around us in a given moment and assert it in a way that rings with truth. Think of the last time you allowed a thought or a stream of ideas to formulate in your mind and you articulated it with the full presence of your being. At such times we can feel the creative energy of our words reverberating in the air that carries them. Many indigenous cultures, past and present, recognise the air, the wind and the human breath as aspects of a sacred, sensuous medium through which they live and have their being. Spoken words are thought to draw their communicative power from this invisible realm, the 'structured breath' that voices the intentions of these spiritual powers. American philosopher David Abram says, 'as the experiential source of both psyche and spirit, it would seem that the air was once felt to be the very matter of awareness, the subtle body of the mind'.[9]

Too much or too little Gemini

So do you think you have too much or too little of this medicine in you? An excess can make you an exceptionally quick and agile thinker, ever responsive and adaptable to changing circumstances, but it can also render you a little unstable. You may experience yourself too much 'in the air', always in transit, never quite embodied in the here and now. This may be indicated in your birthchart if Mercury is especially prominent, or if you have many planets in Gemini. It is also, to some extent, a cultural affliction, with so many of us addicted to our smartphones and other devices that keep us elsewhere, distracting us from the present. To balance this we can learn to meditate, to learn to breathe more consciously and nurture that relationship between breath and spirit. Spend more time in nature, introduce some regularity in your daily rhythm; seek counsel from and dialogue with those who are grounded in their being. You may also benefit from taking definite action on one particular idea or train of thought and keeping faith with it. This is the medicine of Gemini's opposite sign, Sagittarius.

Having too little Gemini or Mercury medicine can make you slow to respond, leaving you stuck in patterns of thought and behaviour, and more easily forgetting the power you have to create your reality through your thoughts and use of language. You will benefit greatly from taking in more air, feeling the air on your skin, remembering that there are stories waiting to be retold, and that in their retelling your life can take on new meaning; new pathways of understanding can open up for you. Breathe deeply of this medicine.

Your word is your bond with the Universe

Our words and the thoughts that inform them do not simply label things that are already there, they also carry a conjuring power which, particularly when given voice, formulates in the air around us and shapes our reality. So let us pay attention to the words we use to get the wheel turning again at this Gemini phase. Pay extra attention to your thoughts, worries and anxieties. If we reinforce a pattern of thinking strongly enough it will manifest as such in our lives. It has been said that worrying is *praying for what you don't want to happen*, and there is truth in this. Imagine that your word is your sacred bond with the Universe; notice if and how you squander your thoughts, waste your language on petty judgements and observations. Begin to check yourself when you notice this happening and realise that you have a choice to start being more mindful, both in the way you manage your thoughts and how you speak. As you do, your reality will change.

Gemini summary

These questions and exercises are designed to help you animate and enliven your relationship with the medicine of Gemini. The questions are designed to stimulate response and reflection. Continue working with your journal and note any insights and inspirations that arise.

CONSIDER THESE QUESTIONS, ASK YOURSELF:

- What are the main dilemmas that preoccupy me and what might be the source of my doubts?

- What language patterns do I get stuck in? Notice any stock phrases that you use repeatedly.

- What do I worry about; in what ways am I praying too hard for what I don't really want?

- In what ways do I engage in too much loose talk?

- What do I gossip and complain about?

NOW CONSIDER THIS:

- How might you re-engage in a dialogue with the spirits of the air in a more imaginative way?

- How could you use language in a more creative way?

- How might you address the world directly, give voice to your intentions?

SUGGESTED EXERCISES AND ACTIVITIES

- Begin a meditation practice. Spend fifteen minutes
  each day paying attention to your breath. As thoughts
  arise, just notice them without getting attached. Keep
  returning to the observation of your breath and relax
  into the practice. Become aware of the spaces
  between thoughts. Imagine you are spring-cleaning
  the airwaves of your mind, becoming a clearer
  channel through which inspiration can speak.

- Articulate in words, as clearly as possible, what you
  want to invite into your life – perhaps a more fulfilling
  job, a new relationship, better health, more recre-
  ational time. Express it in the active, present,
  continuous form of the verb so that it resonates with
  the Universe, as if it is already happening. Start something like this: 'I am enjoying ...', 'I am living ...',
  'I am having ...'. Then turn this into a creative affirma-
  tion or mantra that you can introduce into your daily
  practice.

- Break a habit in the way that you communicate with
  someone in your life. Be more assertive with someone
  who tends to dominate in their conversation with you;
  really listen to someone from who you normally
  'switch off'.

- Avoid gossip and practise disengaging from it. Catch yourself in the same way if you find yourself complaining.

The Fourth Gateway

Cancer

Sun in Cancer period: *20/21 June (Summer Solstice) – 22/23 July*

Symbol: *The Crab/Scarab Beetle*

Motivation: *Cardinal/initiating*

Element (temperament): *Water*

Ruling planet: *Moon*

Body parts ruled: *Breasts, stomach*

Keynote: *I remember. I long to reconnect.*

Version of the truth: *I need to know where it comes from. Does it feel right?*

Medicine: *Nurturance. Protection. Gentleness and care.*

Shadow energy: *Fear. Feeling unsafe. Protectionism. Addictive behaviours.*

Mantra: *I am connected to the source of my being and I remember my origins.*

The transition from Gemini to Cancer

If you have really taken a deep draught of the Gemini medicine your mind will now be alert, agile, inventive and receptive to new possibilities. You might be seeing genuine shifts happening around you, opportunities opening up, people responding to you differently, your word carrying the power of intention. Skilful use of language is a powerful manifestation resource, but Mercury can also trick us into thinking that it's enough on its own. So many fine ideas, projects and self-development programmes become stuck at the cerebral level, bewitched by the cleverness of the linguistic sleight of hand. If you take the language game of life too literally the next transition can be uncomfortable, for we now need to integrate our feelings and turn towards the deep soul of our being. The sign of Cancer returns us to the source of our feelings and to our origins. In this stage of the wheel you will come to know whether your Geminian affirmations are rooted deeply enough in your being; do you feel them at your core? As David Abram says: 'Only if words are felt, bodily presences, like echoes or water-falls, can we understand the power of spoken language to influence, alter, and transform the perceptual world.'[1]

What really matters to you?

Gemini has blessed us with lively, stimulating conversation and provided us with the media through which to stay connected with each other. We are continually updating our communication devices, which we carry around with us wherever we go, and we have a multitude of platforms for information exchange. But beyond all the conversations, emails, texts and tweets, beyond the thoughts and ideas that feed them, what nourishes the deepest core of you? Beyond all those distractions and interruptions to the natural rhythm of your life, what actually feeds your soul? What if the purpose of your life was simply to find your way home? Being by the sea, sitting by a stream or a river, or spending time at a natural spring might give you a sense of this, a sense of being in the flow, memories evoking a feeling of return. This next phase of the wheel invites you to withdraw your attention from the busyness of your everyday interactions and contemplate what it is that you really need. As you pass through the gateway of Cancer now, carry this question in mind: *What really matters to me?*

The realm of water

The fourth (and final) element in the zodiacal round is that of water, and it beckons us into the depths of the psyche. Fire has ignited our spirit, earth has granted us a body and air has awakened our mind; now we turn to water to remember that we are soul. The philosopher Thales, in the sixth century BCE, identified the element of water as the primal stuff of life, the first principle from which all else follows. Evolutionary theory holds that life originated in the oceans and we know that water is the first and primary resource that we human beings need in order to survive. Water holds memory and moves with hypnotic rhythm. It takes us down into the nether realm of soul, and in order to journey further on our way to wholeness, we must now descend like the Sun into the brood of night.

The descent of the solar wheel

The Sun is at its seasonal zenith now, so this may seem like an odd time of year to talk about descent, yet in many traditions this is the time when the Sun God is said to decline towards the Underworld. Cancer is also said to be the gateway of incarnation, the portal through which the human soul takes physical form.[2] At the Summer Solstice the Sun stands still for three days before beginning its own descent on 24 June, the Christian feast day of St John.[3] In Europe there is a tradition, stretching back almost two millennia, that around Midsummer (specifically in England on St John's Eve) people would set fire to a cartwheel and roll it down a hill to a river below. If the flaming wheel made it all the way to the water, it was considered a fortunate omen and promised a good harvest.[4] This solar ritual mimics the Sun's return to the realm of water.

Rhythms and tides

In this meeting of fire and water, the solar yang energy of the seasonal zenith meets its counterpoint, the Moon, ruler of Cancer and carrier of the yin current. In the northern hemisphere we find ourselves deeply immersed in the warm belly of summer, trees pregnant with their sweetening fruits, their roots drawing deep for watery sustenance. Under the guardianship of the Moon, our attention turns inwards (and backwards and downwards); during this phase of the wheel we must remind ourselves what nurtures and nourishes our soul. The movements of the crab and the rhythms of the Moon and tides seem to embody the instinct to turn back towards these fundamental concerns. Crabs often live on the cusp of earth and water, scuttling sideways and backwards with apparent caution, their protective shells covering the soft vulnerable flesh within. In order to grow, the crab must periodically shed its shell and grow another. It rocks with the ebb and flow of the tide, pulled by the ever-waxing and waning Moon, just as the typical Moon-ruled Cancerian will tend to be pulled more than most by their moods and menstrual cycles. Learning to accept the way these tides turn within us, and allowing ourselves to feel these changing rhythms, can help us find our way home.

The downward and inward tug of the soul

The goddess Hera once sent a giant crab to nip the ankles of the Greek hero Heracles (Roman Hercules), while he fought the many-headed hydra. She wanted him to remember his origins and his duty of care to the Great Mother. For Heracles, though, the crab was an unpleasant distraction and he simply crushed the divinely sent creature. Hera then placed the crab in the heavens for its loyalty, to become the constellation we know as Cancer.⁵ It seems an insignificant story, almost an afterthought; yet its subtlety tells us much about this gentle water sign. In this phase of the wheel we feel the past calling us back, and if we are sensitive we will respond in a different way to the Greek hero. Traumatised both by the complex circumstances of his birth and by the unintended violence towards his wife and family, Hercules does not have the capacity to respond to the downward and inward tug of the soul.⁶ He is focused only on conquest and dispatching any obstacles in his path. This medicine teaches us that in our ambitious quest for liberation, atonement and self-realisation, we must remember to integrate the soul's irreconcilable yearning for belonging and continuity.

The Milky Way back home

Hercules's story can also be seen as an inability to relate to the feminine, a theme that was set early in his life. While being wet-nursed by Hera, he bit so hard on her breast that it caused her milk to spurt across the sky, creating the Milky Way, the great cosmic river along which the soul was said to travel between lives. This spectacular band of starlight which stretches across the night sky, formed by the distant light of billions of stars, enables us to observe the extent of our own galaxy. The entry point of human incarnation was said to be where this great starry river crossed the ecliptic, marked in the tropical . zodiac as the gateway of Cancer. If you have ever lain under a starry night sky, far enough from the streetlit world to see the

Milky Way meandering its way above and around you, you may have instinctively asked yourself: *Where do I come from?* The Milky Way that spurts from the breast of the goddess connects us directly to our origins in the starry heavens.

The scarab and the Milky Way

The impressive zodiac ceiling in the late-kingdom Egyptian Temple of Hathor in Dendera shows the goddess Nut arching her body over the images of the zodiac. It depicts Cancer as the first sign, positioned near her womb in the form of a scarab beetle. Both Nut and Hathor have strong associations with the Milky Way, the Great Mother, birth, nurturance and the sustaining of human life.[7] The scarab beetle was considered a symbol of originating creative power, deified by the Egyptians as Khepri, god of the rising Sun. This creature *appears* to reproduce without the need for sexual congress, making it a symbol of originating life. Feeding off the faeces of other animals, the scarab deposits its eggs after they have been rolled into a ball of dung during the space of twenty-eight days – equivalent to one lunar cycle through the zodiac – and directs itself using the Sun, Moon and stars. Remarkably, both beetles and crabs have compound eyes which enable them to make out the stars of the night sky. When the Sun sets, the beetle is guided by the Moon and, according to a recent study, during dark Moon times it navigates by the stars of the Milky Way.[8] The humble scarab is the only creature known to do this, as if somehow it knows the way home to the origin of all life.

What does 'home' mean to you?

Few things in life are more important to us than finding a home, somewhere we can feel safe and secure, and we may spend much of our lives searching for it. What does home mean to you? A place of peace, perhaps, of connection; a place where we are loved unconditionally, a place of warmth and care, a place to return to. We might connect home with the feeling of belonging, of *being at home* within ourselves, surrounded by the natural beauty of the world. For some, home is a garden, a favourite place of sanctuary, of deep and sustaining trust and joy. What does that look like for you? Our actual memory of home may be very far from this ideal, perhaps being a place where we felt isolated, unloved, controlled, violated or abandoned. This betrayal of how home should have been has set in motion a whole series of behaviours that unconsciously replicate the dysfunction we experienced. As adults we often struggle to make a home the way we would like it to be, and this struggle can be a source of deep sadness and grief. Yet most of us can imagine home as it *could* be. The invitation in this phase of the wheel is to nurture that ideal and, in so doing, draw it closer to our lived reality.

A temple that can house the soul

The Greeks have a richly conceived term for home, *oikos*, from which root we derive the term 'eco'. It embraces not only a place, but also an experiential desire for home. Even more profoundly, it refers to the building and caretaking of a temple that could house the soul. Thomas Moore speaks of the experience of enchantment, 'thick in the air', when we are filled with this sense of *oikos*, and how we are 'haunted by its elusiveness' when it is not present.[9] Even if we associate home with a definite place, it is because that place is inhabited by Soul that it feels like home. It is not enough just to be *housed*, for housing alone does not feed the soul; only home can do that.

The sweet spot

I sometimes refer to Cancer as 'the sweet spot' in the zodiac. In Gemini we are outwardly pollinating and flapping our wings; what manifests in the air is exciting, but Cancer returns us to the nest to brood and to the hive where the honey is made. It touches a place within us where we are completely connected to all that is and all that has been, something for which we know there is no substitute. I always welcome this phase of the wheel because it draws me back to the source, to the wellspring, where I can drink deeply of Memory's healing waters, remember where I come from and begin to re-vision what I may have come here for. Spend a moment connecting to that 'sweet spot' within you. Draw from some experience in your memory, or a place you have dreamed of, a place

that you can imagine where you feel completely held, unconditionally loved and nurtured. Go there now, spend a little time there, relax and breathe into it. Let it heal you.

Memory, the mother of the Muses

Memory was more than a concept in ancient times; she was a Greco-Roman goddess, known as Mnemosyne, the mother of the Muses, beloved of poets and artists. We usually think of memory as a 'mental' function for storing times, dates, places, people and events – a record keeper. Yet memories evoke deep feelings; the way we remember something will depend on how we felt at the time and how we feel now. Mnemosyne was no mere archivist. She was endowed with imaginative potency, a spinner of yarns, 'a falsifier of facts and a literaliser of fictions'.[10] So it is with our own memories, which are never just factual accounts of what has happened but rather a collection of mythic strands woven through events and circumstances, conjuring images of the past that our minds quickly assemble into a convincing order. As we observed in Gemini, the stories we weave and reweave about past events become indistinguishable from the events themselves. Patrick Harpur describes memory as the 'form that imagination takes when it wants to impress us with its reality'.[11] Over the years, I have learned to court Mnemosyne with care, connecting with the stories that feed my soul, strengthen my roots and allow the blood of ages to flow through me.

Ancestral roots

When we first meet someone one of the natural questions we ask is 'Where are you from?' We might typically expect an answer that names the village, town, city or country of birth. But what of our tribe? In times past, or in more traditional societies today, the important question is 'To what tribe do you belong, and who are your ancestors?' The signature tune of Cancer is a blood song that flows through us, through our ancestral line, to the very roots of our family trees. At one Cancer workshop of The Alchemical Journey, the group was enquiring into ancestral connections, looking at photos of family members, both living and deceased. As a way of experiencing this, we ventured into a local woodland to connect with the roots of trees. Afterwards, one member of our group, highly animated, shared her experience. While contemplating the relationship between the tree she had been sitting with and her own family tree, she became seized by a profound revelation: *tree roots carry on living and growing beneath the ground, even though we don't see them.* As she shared this, the atmosphere in the room changed, becoming charged with a knowing presence. The meaning of this simple truth struck each one of us, and together we shared a moment of sublime collective understanding. It didn't, of course, solve the metaphysical conundrum of what happens when we die, but it offered each of us a way of remembering and reanimating our relationship to our origins. For a moment, the ancestors became living presences in our midst.

Turning back, remembering

The Greek philosopher Plotinus coined the term *epistrophe*, to describe the desire inherent in all things to 'turn back' towards original guiding principles, their *archai*, or archetypes.[12] One of the most compelling characteristics of the zodiac wheel is that it seems to preserve the integrity of these archetypal images and root metaphors. Often when people come to learn astrology they say it feels more like remembering than learning something new, exposing a 'tacit knowledge' of astrological symbolism that already exists within us.[13] The zodiac is an ancient emblem of the soul and this book is written to foster this capacity that you already have for remembering this stream of ancient wisdom that flows through you. Consider that we are re-entering an imaginal temple, a theatre of archaic memory aides, through which we gently, but definitely, release the potency of the zodiac's living mythology of images and symbols.

The shadow energy of Cancer: unconscious, addictive behaviours

The shadow energy of Cancer tends to revolve around deep-rooted patterns of fear and protectionism which, when overindulged, can be extremely painful and destructive to our well-being. The crab's hard shell protects a vulnerable core, and sometimes we can become so afraid of threats (real or apparent) from outside forces that we hide away from the world or behind inauthentic behaviours. These are founded early in life, when we decided the world wasn't a safe place to be in. Perhaps our childhood circumstances placed us in real physical danger. Some of us may have been violated by a parent or significant elder, some of us abandoned, some smothered by our parents' anxieties. Maybe the person we put all our faith in failed to hold us, suddenly dropped us, or simply wasn't there when we needed them. Who and what we thought we could depend on for unconditional love, care and support turned out to be unreliable and a crucial bond of trust was broken. We don't have the resources to deal with this when we are so young, so we learn to react to threatening situations in ways that will protect us from the excesses of this pain. These reactions get threaded into a very tight weave at these early stages and can be hard to unstitch. We naturally cling to actions and behaviours that are familiar, no matter how uncomfortable or dysfunctional they are. Addicted to the familiarity, we accumulate habits that have us repeat the same cycle of response over and over. We reach for the bottle, the drug, the abusive lover; learn to disengage from or overaccommodate others, making our loved ones wrong. We amass money and possessions, become addicted to sex or self-gratification; we develop strategies of dependency, defensiveness, aggressiveness. And all of this to guard against the exposure of that original wound. Unfortunately, in the process we accrue a far greater amount of suffering.

Too much or too little Cancer

If you are overdependent on Cancer medicine or carry especially pronounced Moon energy, you may tend towards protective and defensive ways of being. You might dwell too much in the past, cling to the family, or the family patterns, in a way that doesn't serve you. You might tend to be overreactive, moody, oversensitive to the monthly lunar cycles, become crabby when you sense any kind of intrusion upon your space. Are you hiding under the covers, not stepping up as much as you could? If so, you could benefit greatly from taking on some of the qualities of Cancer's opposite sign, earthy Capricorn. If you lack much access to Cancerian energy, or if your Moon is weak or challenged in your chart, you may benefit greatly from letting yourself be held, nurtured and nourished by those closest to you. Returning to the bosom of the family, going back to your place of origin, honouring your roots in some way, imagining that deep experience of home; this is good medicine for you. Whether we have too much or too little, at this phase in the wheel we need to learn to pay extra attention to the needs of our so-called *inner child*.

Reparenting your inner child

There is an opportunity in this phase to check these patterns, to realise that you are not bound by them. A part of you is still eternally young, innocent, and close to Spirit, needing nothing more than to be loved and cared for. You can build a sanctuary within your own heart for this inner child of yours. If you can, create a space in your home for them and give them some dedicated time every day. Use a pillow or a soft toy to represent them and, as the parent, hold them as you would hold someone you cherish as much as life itself. Say reassuring things that they long to hear. Move into the role of the child and let yourself become that part of you: cry, laugh, play, shout, ask for what you need; then switch to the parental role and just hold them, listen to them, love them and give them exactly what they need. This is about re-establishing trust. Keep moving between the roles until you feel that some sense of trust is established; then, as the parent, make a final promise to the child that they are loved; reassure them that you are always there for them. If you develop this as a practice, they will start to believe you and you will gain easier access to your joy and creativity.

Cancer summary

Spend time during this stage of the wheel connecting more deeply with your feelings. You can engage with the following enquiries and suggested activities and share your intimate reflections in your journal.

CONSIDER THESE QUESTIONS, ASK YOURSELF:

- What does home mean to you?

- Where (or in what situations) do you feel most 'at home'?

- Where is your 'sweet spot'?

- What feelings or experiences are you addicted to, in a way that you can't control?

SUGGESTED EXERCISES AND ACTIVITIES

- If you haven't done so already, designate a place in your living environment as your sanctuary or sacred space, where you can connect with your deep self.

- Practise the Reparenting Your Inner Child exercise outlined above.

- Identify a habitual behaviour and notice when you do it, and in what circumstances. Practise responding differently.

- Listen to soothing music, take a long soak in a bath, spend time by the sea. Practise finding your own natural rhythm of intake and outflow.

- Visit a local spring and spend time there connecting to the blessing of water drawn from its original source.

The Fifth Gateway

Leo

Sun in Leo period: *22/23 July – 22/23 August*

Symbol: *The Lion*

Motivation: *Fixed/establishing and maintaining*

Element (temperament): *Fire*

Ruling planet: *Sun*

Body parts ruled: *Heart, spine*

Keynote: *I create. I produce. I show.*

Version of the truth: *Does it have heart? Is it authentic?*

Medicine: *Self-expression. Confidence. Generosity of spirit. Heart-fullness.*

Shadow energy: *Excessive pride. Ego-centrism. Not seeing one's own shadow.*

Mantra: *I am as I am, and I shine from the centre of my being.*

The transition from Cancer to Leo

If we are to progress on our journey we need to leave the safety of the nest and answer the call of the heart to grow and individuate. If we have made the journey home within ourselves and found nourishment, we are ready. If we have revisited and made peace with some aspect of our past, created a place of sanctuary within, spent time at the wellspring, suckled on the breast of the life-giving goddess, we are now strong and vital enough to step out on our own and claim our rightful destiny.

In Leo, the second fire sign on the wheel, we enter the most truly heroic phase of the cycle. We move from the breast to the heart, from mother to father, from Moon to Sun, from reflective silver light to eternal golden light. To make that transition we need courage. We are shifting from the crab to the lion, from a hard-shelled, vulnerable creature of the tides to one at the head of the food chain who must live up to the billing 'King of Beasts'. The contrast could not be more stark; it involves a monumental shift of energy and perspective. At the same time, it is an entirely natural transition, for it is now time for the child to become an adult. It is a rite of passage.

Risking your heart

There are times when we must stretch ourselves beyond what is comfortable. What does your safe ground look like? Where would you locate that familiar territory in your life that nurtures you but doesn't necessarily challenge you? Sometimes we have to push ourselves to get out there. Are you prepared to risk your heart? There is a crossing of a threshold from the known to the unknown and it calls forth a more daring aspect of our character. Recall a time when you made that crossing and really showed up, revealed something true and authentic about yourself. Perhaps you stood up in front of an audience for the first time, stepped out onto a stage or exhibited your creative work. We risk being shamed, judged or rejected when we expose that golden, authentic part of us, yet to keep it hidden is the greatest risk of all. We need to feel emotionally connected enough within ourselves in order to take that next step in the process of individuation, but if we overindulge that need for safety we may fail to grasp the invitation for our heart to shine when the opportunity presents itself. So as the wheel turns again and we enter the gateway of Leo, draw upon your courage and your commitment to growth and ask yourself this question: *What does my heart want to express?*

Answering the heroic call

Arthur may only be a child with no apparent aptitude for warriorship, but he is the one destined to draw the sword from the stone and claim his royal birthright. Luke Skywalker may love his home planet Tatooine and be reluctant to leave behind everything that has supported him, but when his heart hears the call of his destiny, he must answer it. As in many hero myths, young Skywalker is destined to redeem the failings of his own father in order to become fully himself. In Cancer, we needed to restore trust in the feminine and make our peace with the Mother. In Leo we must restore the integrity of the masculine image within us and, wherever it is called for, address the father wound that we all carry.

Fire in the heart

The medicine we look for from our fathers is different to that which we depend upon from our mothers. We look to our fathers to set an example for how to live an authentic life of honour, dignity and integrity. Whatever our gender, the archetypal masculine urge within us seeks to be authentically recognised, realised and expressed. We want our father to be our hero and our king, so that we can fully realise what is heroic and sovereign within ourselves. A young boy needs a father figure who can model this, both challenging him and inspiring him with qualities towards which he can aspire. A young girl needs both an inspiration and protector, someone to admire and help establish the boundaries of a strong self. In so many cases, though, our fathers were not able to live up to this high expectation. Maybe their fires burned too strong, manifesting as tyrannical aggression and rage; maybe we were left with an image of a weak-hearted coward, a heart that failed to catch fire at all. More than likely you experienced something in between or a paradoxical mix of the two. This can be just as painful, as one of the things we look for from the father archetype is consistency, a true and faithful heart in which we can trust, and this is the journey for each of us as we strive to manifest our authentic selves.

The lion Sun king

The lion has always been associated with dignity and rulership and is one of the most familiar cultural symbols of sovereignty. The brightest star in the Leo constellation, Regulus, sits almost exactly on the ecliptic, directly in the path of the Sun, giving it great symbolic power. It is placed right in the heart of the lion figure. The male lion's impressive mane has an obvious resemblance to the Sun's rays, and the Sun is said to be in its dignity in this sign. The Sun gives us the power to shine; its radiant light and power inspires the life force to grow, to realise the destiny imprinted at birth, in its seed. That seed was sown in the first fire sign, Aries; now it is ready to mature into its adult potential. The spark of cardinal fire is the impulse of the Mars-inspired warrior, who presents himself now before the stable authority of the sovereign ruler to be exalted.[1]

The heart of summer

The Sun enters the royal sign of Leo around 22/23 July, the hottest period of the year in the northern hemisphere, a time of fierce heat, particularly at the Mediterranean latitudes. In summer, fruits ripen, fields of golden wheat and corn sway elegantly in the breeze and sunflowers turn their proud faces towards the Sun. The work can wait until it is time to bring in

the harvest in Virgo. This is more a time of recreation and festivity, which better suits the Leo temperament, and which is evident in the behaviour of the male lion, who seems to spend most of his time relaxing while the females do all the work! We will turn our attention now to the harder-working, more intensely focused lioness, because she reveals an important side of this sign which we must integrate.

The power of the lioness

Ancient myths from cultures enduring the hottest summers carry warnings about the destructive power of the Sun and, by extension, the sign of Leo. The hunting lioness was venerated as a war deity in ancient Egypt. She conferred courage on the warrior, yet could be brutal in her destructive power. The lion-headed goddess Sekhmet was known for her fierce, fiery nature, burning passionately and consistently with the scorching heat of the midday sun, and the Egyptians likely would have associated her with the hottest phase of the year. A daughter of the Sun God, Ra, her hot breath was said to have created the desert. Her name is from *sekhem*, meaning power, and she is sometimes referred to as the 'one before whom evil trembles'.[2] In one of the most famous stories attributed to her, she is dispatched by Ra, towards the end of his earthly reign, to destroy the mortals who have conspired against him. In so doing her latent fury is unleashed; her blood-lust cannot be sated even after the battle is won. In a desperate attempt to soothe her, Ra pours out beer dyed with red ochre, which Sekhmet mistakes for blood. She gets so drunk that she gives up on the slaughter and returns in shame, peacefully, to Ra.[3] Many leonine or solar myths carry destructive themes like this; they seem to imply that a respect must be paid to the Sun, lest it should burn up humanity.

Inner strength

The balanced energy of the Sun is expressed through the benevolent Egyptian cat goddess, Bast, a protectress and goddess of healing. She is sometimes seen as the peaceful aspect of Sekhmet.[4] As River and Gillespie have pointed out, there is often an overemphasis on the male lion as 'king of the beasts', and a neglect of the lioness who is actually the pride's great provider and protector. Her blend of power and playfulness is indicative of the free flow of her sexual energy, commanding respect while also carrying a moist sweetness.[5] Different cultures often show a lioness as the companion of the goddess; it is a symbol of strength and confidence. The wild raging nature of the lion has been brought under control and that power has been assumed by the woman who is fully resident in her own power. The eighth trump of the Tarot, Strength, depicts a female figure in communion with a lion, who seems altogether peaceful in her presence.[6] The cultivation of this inner strength offers us a potent opportunity for transformation at this stage of the journey.

The path of the solar hero

For the ancient Greeks the constellation of Leo is the Nemean Lion, which Heracles (Roman Hercules) must kill in his cycle of labours (traditionally his first). Stripped of his birthright and cursed by Hera, Heracles is seized by a madness which causes him to commit atrocious acts in his youth. Shamed by his actions, he is compelled to atone for his past and undertake his twelve zodiacal labours, to fulfil his destiny and become the 'Glory of Hera' that befits his name. Heracles is a classic Leonine figure, wearing the pelt and headdress of a lion. The Nemean lion has become a despotic, terrorising force of nature, whose brutality knows no bounds, and whose pelt is impenetrable.[7] Heracles is forced to bide his time and cannot overcome it until he has fully embodied his own lion nature.

Hercules is a solar hero on a quest of self-realisation. In contrast to the more soul-oriented Odysseus (Roman Ulysses), he is associated with the direct, upward path of Spirit.[8] He is on a quest to conquer the forces of darkness, and he brings things up into the light of conscious awareness, dazzling us with the power of his solar fire, eventually succeeding in his quest for immortality. James Hillman argues that Hercules has become the archetypal hero of the modern ego and its desire for personal recognition.[9] The ego's impetus is to break free from its mother's breast and launch itself into heroic action. It gives us the strength, independence and willpower needed to break the bonds of dependency and overcome the challenges we face in the world. Its direction of travel is upwards and outwards towards liberation, superficially similar to the way Spirit moves to ultimately free itself from the confines of the body. When this is expressed authentically, with respect for the greater cycle of life and a honouring of each and every aspect of the wheel, it can liberate us from the chains of fear, help reconnect us with the divine source of our being. This is the great possibility in the Herculean path. The ever-present danger, however, is that the soul gets abandoned along the way. This usually involves a neglect of feminine wisdom, a failure to respect the Underworld, and a loss of perspective when it comes to dealing with the cycles of death and rebirth. This brings us to the core of the Leo shadow energy.

The shadow

In order to attempt an authentic expression of Leonine energy, we must first understand its shadow manifestation. I invite you to indulge this fantasy for a moment. Imagine the Sun beating down on you one hot summer's day. Imagine it lighting you up inside, making you feel as if it were shining *just for you*. It is your moment in the Sun. Now consider the dark, literal shadow that lies beside you on the ground. Whichever way you turn, it turns with you, there is no escape; and while you remain cast in this brilliant light, it remains; the brighter the light, the more intense and clearly defined that shadow will be. So it is as we enter close to the heart of the solar hero. We are tempted ever more by the power it offers us, the apparent self-importance it appears to confer. As that bright light shines upon us, revealing our divine gift, we may start to feel that we have been uniquely chosen to represent the Sun's glory. At this point, we could go one of three ways.

The Leo shadow of hubris

Going against the will of the gods, against the cycles of nature, thinking you can bypass the doorway of death, even attempting to raise the dead as Hercules, Orpheus and Apollo's son Asclepius once did; these were the sins of hubris in Greek myth, and carried the greatest punishment. If you are over-represented in the sign of Leo, or if the Sun in your horoscope is overexposed, there may be good medicine for you in the following story. Helios, the god of the Sun, would drive his solar chariot across the sky each day; at dusk each evening, his energy spent, he would dive into the waters of all-encircling Oceanus. As he travelled through the nether realm he would be replenished, his fiery power recharged through the passage of night. Helios had a son, Phaethon, who was his greatest pride, and one day, gripped with the full generosity of his heart, the solar deity offered his son anything he wanted. To his horror, the boy asked to be allowed to take the reins of his father's powerful steeds and drive the chariot of the Sun for one day. His father could not go back on his word, and Phaethon was resolute in his choice. The consequences were disastrous; the boy did not have the experience, mettle or strength of character to steady the horses, nor did he understand that the Sun draws its power from its night-time passage. And so it was that the chariot came crashing to Earth in a mighty fireball, destroying everything in its path.

Rites of passage and the stroppy teenager

Phaethon's story points to the shadow of uninitiated youth. Leo marks the transition from child to adult in the zodiac wheel, when our hormones are stirred and we become sexually active. In traditional societies, at this time a boy would be taken from his mother by the men of the village and put through a gruelling initiation ritual into manhood; a young girl would be initiated by the womenfolk when she first began to menstruate. This has been identified by anthropologists as a threefold process of *separation* from the family environment; *transition*, often involving some form of sacred, physical wounding; and *reincorporation* into the community.[10] Western religions have their versions of this, but in our predominantly secular modern societies, rite-of-passage ceremonies are notably absent. Without a strong community of elders and role models to act as guides, teenagers, in the main, have to fend for themselves and make up their own rites, whether through gang membership, self-harming, wanton sexual experimentation or rebellion against anything that smacks of authority. This missing initiation at such a crucial time of transition often haunts us into adulthood, and in this phase of the wheel we can do something to address it. In Cancer, we needed to regain trust in our nurturing parent; here we need to regain trust in the parent who was supposed to initiate us and guide us into adulthood. As adults we need to accept how angry the teenage part of us still is, and create space for them to vent their frustration and rage. It's no good giving them the keys to the solar chariot to compensate for how little time we have to spend with them. It's no good making them wrong for their anger or lack of judgement, or trying to placate them. We need to really listen to them, with compassion and strong holding.

The Leo shadow of cowardice

This is the second way we could go. With the spotlight upon us, we may shy away with ruddy-faced embarrassment. *Who me?... No, you must have the wrong person.* This failure to show up puts us in mind of the cowardly lion in the *Wizard of Oz.* Everyone can see he is a lion, but he is clearly a disappointment, both to himself and to others; he lacks courage and cannot stand in his sovereignty. He is trying to be a lion, trying to impress, but it is not authentic. If we lack access to Leo energy, or if our astrological Sun is hidden or somehow afflicted in the birthchart, our journey is one of rediscovering our true heart and learning to roar again. The lion's transformation in the story occurs when the wizard authenticates him by awarding him a badge of courage. In this act of blessing from an elder, he is finally recognised for who and what he is. This leads us to the third and most authentic way of expressing this energy.

Standing authentically in the light of who you are

We have a tradition at the Leo stage of *The Alchemical Journey* where we lay a red carpet down the middle of the hall and each participant gets to walk along it in turn, accompanied by a piece of uplifting music designed to help them rise to the occasion of having their moment in the Sun. We call it the Big Cat Walk. At the end of the red carpet is a throne on which the person is crowned king or queen. Each member of the group says something that acknowledges what they perceive as that person's sovereign nature, authenticating what they see as the light shining from their heart. It is a powerful piece of sacred theatre; for some people, this may be the first time they have ever been acknowledged in such a way.

What we learned from these experiences is that what scares us most is not necessarily our darkness, but rather, the dazzling light of our potential brilliance. A crowning inspiration of this stage of the wheel is encapsulated in a well-known piece of writing from Marianne Williamson. She wisely points out that playing small offers no great service to the world, that diminishing the true nature of who we are so that others don't feel insecure around us, is no great signature of enlightenment.

Let this fiery medicine inspire you, and find within it the authentication of your true heart:

> We are all meant to shine, as children do. We were
> born to make manifest the glory of God within us.
> It's not just in some of us; it's in everyone. And as

we let our own light shine, we unconsciously give other people permission to do the same.[11]

It is your gift to give

In the Taurus phase, we identified our natural talents and resources, those that we are given and can be thankful for. In Leo, we get to offer our talents as gifts. The very nature of a gift is that it is something we give away to the world, but not in a way that diminishes us or depletes our resources. When we are true to ourselves, we give authentically from the heart and our energy is continually replenished and renewed. A true gift is an expression of our joy, born of our willingness to stay connected to the creative source of the Sun. When we give from that place, the gift returns to us and in an ever-expanding cycle of joy.

Leo summary

Spend time during this fifth stage of the wheel connecting with your heart and enquiring as to what it is that makes you authentically you. Notice when you are being yourself and how different that feels from when you're pretending to be something you are not.

CONSIDER THESE QUESTIONS:

Ponder these questions about yourself and ask three people who know you well for their opinions.

- What is my special gift to the world?

- In what ways am I playing small and not stepping into the glory of who I really am?

- In what ways do I try too hard to make an impression?

- How do others respond when I am authentically shining my light in the world?

SUGGESTED EXERCISES AND ACTIVITIES

- Write down all the things that make you who you are, that make you shine.

- Watch a heroic movie and put yourself in the shoes of the central character.

- Practise being generous towards those around you. Give of yourself, with all of your heart.

- Imagine there is fiery light radiating from your heart. For a period of time each day when you are out in the world, imagine your aura and field of influence expanding beyond your physical body, touching the people around you.

The Sixth Gateway

Virgo

Sun in Virgo period: *22/23 August – 22/23 September*

Symbol: *The Virgin*

Motivation: *Mutable/adapting and transforming*

Element (temperament): *Earth*

Ruling planet: *Mercury*

Body part ruled: *Intestines*

Keynote: *I will choose, when I am ready.*

Version of the truth: *Does it work? Is it essential? Is it of service?*

Medicine: *Discernment. Embodied choice.*

Shadow energy: *Puritanism. Narrow-mindedness. Hypochondria.*

Mantra: *I discern what is most essential to my well-being and it becomes my practice.*

The transition from Leo to Virgo

If you have taken on the power of the Leo medicine you may feel very expanded now. Perhaps you sense the call of destiny in your heart, a spirit fire that raises you up and makes you feel as if you could be anything and achieve anything with your life. The Force is with you! But we have only completed the fifth stage of the wheel, and this energy must now be grounded. In the zodiac wheel, fire is necessarily always followed by earth. Just as Taurus followed Aries, so Leo must now yield to practical, earthy Virgo. At first this can feel like quite a comedown. We have generated a huge amount of energy, but the light of our expanded vision and the heat of our awakened passion must now be channelled, filtered and applied in concrete, manageable and sustainable ways. Otherwise we risk losing touch with reality, getting carried away with ourselves and becoming too big for the world we inhabit. We are ripe now, as fruit ready to be picked, fully grown as golden wheat ready to be harvested, mature sexual beings full of power and vitality. When Luke Skywalker becomes aware of the Force, he thinks he can conquer everything, but as yet, he has no control over it and it is in Virgo that the hero's training must begin. Having been authenticated, we must now be tested, develop daily practices to cultivate our gifts, hone the essence of our authentic selves, and not waste or abuse the creative potential that has awakened within us. Any aspirations of immortality we may have at this stage are premature; the laws of nature dictate that we must be cut down in our prime.

Feeding the goose

What is it like for you to step back into your daily life when the performance is over, to go back to the drawing board after a creative process has ended, or to clean up after the party? How do you deal with the ordinariness of everyday existence? In Leo, we have had a glimpse of the goose that lays the golden egg, and that goose is your true and authentic heart. So now that you have acknowledged the potential of that, it is time to consider how you feed the goose and what you feed her with. How do you best honour that gold-producing part of you? What practices can you develop that serve the grand production of your own life? If the medicine of Leo has shown you the importance of showing up as your authentic self, Virgo now demands your humility and dedication to that. Remember that glorious moment we had in the Sun? We don't just want that to be a one-off event, a flash in the pan; we need to integrate it into our lives so that it becomes second nature to us. So how do you sustain your capacity for gold-making so that you can continue to produce and perform with vitality and consistency? The wheel has now reached one of its most crucial turning points, and as you enter this gateway, hold in mind this question: *Who and what am I here to serve?*

The harvest goddess

The Sun enters the zodiacal sign of Virgo around 22 August and as it does we enter into one of the deepest mysteries of the astrological year. Virgo is perhaps the most misunderstood and underestimated sign in the zodiacal wheel, one that needs liberation from popular misconceptions if we are to activate the necessary transformation that this critical phase of the wheel demands. The heavenly constellation of Virgo depicts a woman, usually winged, holding a sheaf of wheat or ear of corn in her hand. Her alpha star is Spica, very close to the Sun's path on the ecliptic, a blessed star, bestowing great beneficence. She is generally seen as Demeter (Roman Ceres), the harvest goddess, a much-revered figure of great power and authority, responsible for the fecundity and fertility of the earth. Though greatly honoured and respected in agricultural societies, Virgo is now popularly portrayed as sexless, a domestic servant, administrator and general nit-picker. How can she have fallen from grace in this way? It probably reflects the severely diminished standing of the feminine in our society, particularly within the Christian era, and the lack of reverence in the modern age for Mother Nature. So let us attempt to recast Virgo here as the goddess she really is, a more authentic expression of her true nature as an experienced mistress of purification, discernment, wit and choice.

The only 'free' woman in the sky

There are three female human figures in the Greek sky, and two of them are in chains; Cassiopeia is chained to her queenly throne, and her daughter Andromeda to a rock, awaiting a hero to save her. This says much about the patriarchal nature of Greco-

Roman culture, and within this context it is very significant that Virgo is the only female figure, among the star constellations, who remains free. Even the Greeks dared not chain their precious harvest goddess, and she is the clearest representation of sovereign feminine authority in the sky. The goddess has many facets; as well as being the fecund Earth Mother, she is also the sacred virgin, ritually purified and ready to receive the seed of life; in both roles she epitomises fertility and bounty. Older renderings of the term 'virgin' mean something different than they do today; they referred to a woman who was free, not bound or possessed by any man. Her sexuality was sacred and she was a mistress unto herself, fully aware of her own worth and in control of her own body. This is very different from our modern understanding of the term virgin, which is taken to mean a sexually inexperienced woman (the term was only later applied to men) or a woman who has had a vow of celibacy imposed upon her. This important distinction places the emphasis on a woman's right to remain independent and free of male control. Virginity was a spiritual practice of sacred sexuality, having more to do with rites of purification, which may have involved a woman consciously abstaining from sexual relations for a period of time, while cultivating sexual energy within. As such, a virgin always retained the right to choose when and with whom to express her sexual nature.

Virgin birth

The possibility that Mary gave birth to Christ through the act of parthenogenesis is rarely taken seriously today except by those of devout Christian faith. We can be fairly sure, however, that the belief in the possibility of virgin birth was widespread in the ancient world, long before Mary's miraculous conception. Marguerite Rigoglioso's extensive research into the subject has shown that before they were made into the wives, sisters and daughters of male gods, goddesses like Gaia, Hera, Athena, Artemis and Demeter were worshipped as creatrix beings, 'sovereign and inviolable', believed to have given birth without the need of a male. Specialised virgin priestesshoods were established in Greece and Rome, where women would attempt to conceive in non-ordinary ways as an elevated form of spiritual practice, anticipating the birth of a special type of being.[1] Mary and Jesus follow in the line of Isis and Horus, Anahita and Mithra,[2] among others, as religious instances of parthenogenesis. The implication of Rigoglioso's research is that these 'miracle' births would have come about as a result of the woman perfecting some kind of sexual alchemy. In Christianity, this idea of sacred sexual practice has been replaced by a far more passive concept of sacred celibacy, with the apparent innocence and uninitiated purity of the iconic Virgin Mary becoming the archetypal standard for Christian women to live up to. This image of the sexless virgin replaced the virgin goddesses of the old religions, and female sexuality became shamed and repressed. I am giving this issue attention here partly because it is an important aspect of the origins of this sign, but also to balance Old *and* New Age spiritual assumptions of the creative force being solely male-gendered, as it is in most Western religions. As much as Leo directs us towards the image of an all-powerful creat*or*, Virgo points us to an equally powerful creat*rix*.

Cultivating the power of your essence

The Virgo phase of the wheel addresses the need that we all have to withdraw our energy from outward concerns and to cultivate the power of inner spiritual, sexual and physical essence. In this phase we develop a sensitivity to our inner workings, the workings of the body, in its raw, wild nature. Just as our Leonine experiences have helped us realise and express our confidence and creative potential, so Virgo now sets us to the task of its refinement. We can draw upon the power of the goddess here to turn our spontaneous creative impulses into useful, sustainable practices that serve the greater good. Here we strip away our indulgences, hone our creative practices and transform our promises into everyday miracles. The first earth sign, Taurus, presented us with the fertile potential of the good earth; now Virgo realises that potential as it brings in the harvest. It is the separating of the wheat from the chaff; the golden wheat of our golden selves now needs to be handled, worked and transformed into the food that nourishes a community.

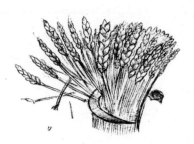

The mysteries of Eleusis

Such ideas form the basis of the oldest of the agrarian mystery traditions, the Eleusinian rites of Demeter and Persephone, practised for over a thousand years until the fourth century BCE. They bear the hallmarks of zodiacal initiation, an imitation of an archetypal drama that mirrors the seasonal cycle of the year. Persephone, beloved daughter of Demeter, is abducted by Hades, Lord of the Underworld, and taken into his realm as his consort and queen. In her grief, Demeter withdraws from Mount Olympus and turns her back on the world, abandoning her duties as the goddess of fertility and laying waste to the earth. Zeus, with half his powers diminished, orders that Persephone be returned; but because she has tasted of the pomegranate fruit of the Underworld, she can only return above ground for part of the year. She does so in the spring, and in the joyful reunion of mother and daughter, fertility is restored to the land. In the autumn she returns to Hades' realm, and as Demeter's grief returns, so nature's green mantle withers and dies. The observation and annual re-enactments of these mystery rites was believed to be crucial to hold society and the whole human race together. The Lesser Mysteries were conducted in the spring at Agra, in Athens, and were purifying and preparatory in nature. We know that they were undertaken by the zodiacal hero Hercules, and were said to be for his own purification so that he could success- fully enter the Underworld. The initiate would have found the rites unsettling, as their aim was to purge them of unhealthy levels of sexual energy, along with distracting thoughts and emotions. Typically a year and a half was devoted to the Lesser

Mysteries before one could partake of the Greater Mysteries; these were held in the autumn in Eleusis, being inaugurated in mid-September, while the Sun was in Virgo.[3]

Body wisdom

Virgo is ruled by Mercury, who is the Greek Hermes, so once again, as in Gemini, we find ourselves in the domain of the wily magician, whose skill and cunning knits together the fabric of life into a seamless dance. We experience a very different side of Hermes as intellect gets woven together with bodily instinct and the acute, observant responses of which our animal selves are capable.

Animals are highly attuned to their surroundings, sensuously alert to every wild call, change of rhythm, unusual texture, musky scent, rustle of leaves underfoot and each tiny flap of wings. In some of us this ability is more naturally developed, while for the rest of us we need to learn to identify and engage with changes in our bodily experience, rather than just changes in our mental field. We might carry strong Gemini medicine, being quick and bright-minded, clever in our dealings with other humans, able to conjure words that alter perspectives, and use language to advance our interests. But in Virgo we must coax out a more embodied way of knowing, the intelligence and language borne of the earth itself. Artemis, virgin goddess of the hunt, can be an inspiration here, being at one with her animal nature and fiercely guarding her independence and her wild freedom. The Greek goddess Metis also embodies this older understanding, often called cunning wisdom, the ability to respond to small changes in one's environment with discerning wit and skill. Metis is swallowed whole by Zeus; nine months later the next goddess of wisdom, Athene, is born from his head.[4] She is the patron and protector of Odysseus, who along with his wife Penelope really exemplify this metic intelligence.

Odysseus and Penelope

Odysseus was the smartest of all the male heroes, with an intelligence matched only by his wife Penelope. There are a multitude of examples of the great wandering hero of the Odyssey being able to respond to the situations he finds himself in with extraordinary agility of both mind and body. A master of strategy, his ruse of the Trojan horse eventually brings victory to the Greeks in the Trojan War, and on his much-blighted journey home his sharp observances get him out of some very tricky situations. Meanwhile, at home on Ithaca, with Odysseus assumed dead, Penelope is keeping her many suitors at bay with her cunning. In order to appease her admirers, she promises that she will take a new husband, but only when she has finished weaving a burial shroud for Odysseus's father, Laertes. So she weaves by day to the satisfaction of the suitors, but then unpicks her work by night, so the shroud is never finished.[5]

The weaving of fate

Weaving itself carries an embodied intelligence, and in many indigenous cultures the activity has a cosmological dimension. The meshing together of the masculine weft with the feminine warp is simultaneously an intertwining of sky and earth, the meeting of opposites necessary for the ongoing dance of creation.[6] Weaving also underscores many ideas about fate and destiny. The *norns* and *valkyries*, for example, female deities who oversee human destiny in Teutonic myth, continually spin the flax and weave the tapestry of life.[7] Fate was not seen as something fixed, but 'as a steady, ongoing process, only fully completed at the end of a lifetime'.[8] The web of fate, known as the *Wyrd*, was believed to set in motion the patterns of life, and yet imposed no ultimate design upon it. It was through one's active participation in the ritual activities of *wyrd*, in the ongoing, everyday weave of life, that the course of that life was determined. A person's destiny was seen as an active co-creation with this web.[9] Pre-existing conditions may set the course and direction of a person's life, but our ability to respond to those conditions determines how that life unfolds, the ever-present potential for transforming the grit into gold.

Everyday magic

Mercury and Metis embed their magic in the everyday details of life that we so easily miss whenever our attention wanders from the delicate intricacies of the moment. Our task in Virgo is to properly engage with our physicality and the web of existence that extends from that. Simple but definite actions assist us in this; to sweep clean, to purify, to polish, to sharpen, to distil, to discern, to ritually observe; above all, to find an inner stillness within these mindful acts as we perfect the ordinary tasks of life. This is a time to clear the clutter, organise your space more efficiently; notice where you've expanded and accumulated things beyond what is manageable, where things are piling up; practise simplifying your life. Introduce more regularity and repetition into your everyday life, be more respectful of time and your body's daily rhythms. Through this, you actually open up the possibility of transcending those same ritual structures and entering a more sublime state of consciousness where you begin to penetrate the weave of life itself. This is the fertile ground within which transformation can occur.

Wax on, wax off

Every year on *The Alchemical Journey*, we show a clip from the 1970s' rite-of-passage film, *The Karate Kid*, in which a young American wannabe is trained by a Japanese Zen master so that he can stand up to a local bully. The boy is full of Leonine charm and bravado, but he is soon brought down to earth. In one classic sequence he is set a series of menial tasks: waxing his teacher's car, painting his garden fence, sanding the floor. 'Wax on, wax off,' his teacher insists. This goes on for days; the boy can see no apparent connection to karate and thinks he is being taken for a ride so that the old man can get his household chores done. His frustration turns to revelation in an extraordinary scene when his teacher shows him that in the embodiment of these repetitive actions he has actually learned a series of powerful karate moves which are now second nature to him. First his teacher authenticates him and builds his confidence, his essential golden nature, then shows him how to harvest that gold.

'Wax on, wax off', as a mindful practice of repeated actions, is the essence of Virgo medicine, so find your own version of it, and think of it as the daily caretaking of your zodiac soul.

The Virgo shadow energy: puritanism

The Virgo ideals of sacred sexuality, purification and choice have been twisted by patriarchal religions. Western cultures are strongly influenced by the historical repression of women, puritanism and the Protestant work ethic, through which we are indoctrinated to abstain from joy and pleasure and to work hard every day to ensure our salvation. Control of society, control of emotion and suppression of desire have thus become a major part of the Virgo shadow. We also grow up with unhealthy ideals around perfection, and unrealistic standards for pure and good lives, while having to deny significant aspects of our human expression. Poor body image is one consequence of this, leading to an increase in eating disorders and psychological complexes around physical appearance.

Too much or too little Virgo

When this medicine dominates our lives to the exclusion of other perspectives, it can make us narrow-minded, pedantic and overly critical of others. We become controlling in the way we manage our environment, intolerant of different ways of arranging things around us, even to the point of obsession in the way we try to keep everything 'just so'. We can worry to excess about our body and our health, even becoming hypochondriacal; we can become so focused on work, on *getting it right* that we forget to nurture our relationships with the things that bring us joy. If so, a good dose of Pisces medicine (Virgo's opposite sign) can help us loosen up and expand our horizons a little! When we are under-represented in Virgo, we may not be discriminating enough, and we may neglect to develop our embodied awareness. We may find it harder to stay focused, or be disciplined enough to engage in any regular practices. Cultivating practical and life skills can help us feel more at home in the everyday world. If you feel you are weak in Virgo energy, pay more attention to your bodily wisdom; be mindful to integrate the suggested enquiries and daily practices into your life.

Virgo medicine: choice and discernment

Making a choice is a powerful thing to do, yet so often we don't fully commit to our choices as we make them; we hedge our bets, keep our options open, don't risk too much. As such, the energy that often accompanies these choices is weak. In

Gemini we sought answers on the wind and in the power of language. Now we need to trust that our body knows what to do. If we can allow ourselves to be moved by that, our choices will carry the power and intention of that embodied knowing. For this we need to connect to our physical being, the earth and the innate intelligence that arises from both. By withdrawing our energy from concerns about how we look, or how our choices will appear to others, we are better able to make concrete decisions. Let your body be your guide, and let wise discernment be your medicine.

Virgo summary

Spend time during this sixth stage of the wheel developing a daily practice that connects you more with your body and be mindful of your sensuous connection to your surroundings. You can engage with the following enquiries and suggested activities.

CONSIDER THESE QUESTIONS, ASK YOURSELF:

- How often in your daily life are you listening to cues from your body? How much do you trust its intelligence when making choices?

- How mindful are you of the details of your everyday life?

- Are there areas of life where you are being too small-minded or getting bogged down in detail, trying to work things out too much in your mind?

SUGGESTED ACTIVITIES AND PRACTICES

- Practise bringing more awareness and presence to simple everyday tasks.

- Create a more mindful sense of order in your personal space. Pick out specific things: items of clothing, books, personal belongings. Decide what to keep and what to pass on, using your discernment to determine: (a) Does it bring me joy? (b) Do I choose to keep this in my life? (c) Does it want to be in my life? (d) How essential is it to my life?

- Develop some form of embodied, mindful practice. Something as simple as a daily walk in nature where you stay present and observant to everything you see around you and notice your body's responses.

- Learn a new skill, or develop an existing one: something that draws on your body wisdom, has a repetitive, rhythmic or ritual element.

The Seventh Gateway

Libra

Sun in Libra period: *22/23 September – 22/23 October*

Symbol: *The Scales*

Motivation: *Cardinal/initiating*

Element (temperament): *Air*

Ruling planet: *Venus*

Body part ruled: *Kidneys*

Keynote: *I consider. I am because we are.*

Version of the truth: *Is it beautiful? Does it produce harmony? Will it bring peace?*

Medicine: *Consideration. Suspending judgement. The art of balance.*

Shadow energy: *Vanity. Overaccommodation of others. Vacillation.*

Mantra: *I come in peace, I walk in beauty and I choose the middle path.*

The transition from Virgo to Libra

If you have absorbed the Virgo medicine, you are now more embodied and self-contained, and you will have put your house in order. The first six signs enable us to gain a certain mastery of ourselves, so that now we are ready to enter the social and ethical world of relationships. This requires us to look up from our workaday lives, lay down our cutting tools for a while and recognise our inevitable, unavoidable related-ness to others. No human being is an island. We are irresistibly attracted to one another, and we cannot ever really know ourselves without having another to act as a mirror for us. We are asked now to bear witness to who we are and how we have developed to this point; for while the productive phase of a particular cycle may be over, its moral charge remains. It is this that must be measured, and the balance sought, in the *apparently* impartial light of reason.

A question of balance

As we make this shift from Virgo to Libra we are moving our attention from the practical concerns associated with the perfecting of our material existence towards a more idealistic appreciation of harmony and relationship. In order to do this, we need to create some space in our lives. To what extent are you working too hard, worrying excessively about your health, or trying too much to control situations in your life? Are you resting enough, giving yourself time for reflection and contemplation? As the sculptor, you have been busily chipping away, trying to perfect the masterpiece of your life. Now it is time to step back and appreciate its form, assess its elegance, pay attention to the question of balance. Are you allowing yourself time to appreciate the beauty around you? Are you giving enough attention to your relationships and spending enough time with those you love? Libra is an air sign and as we enter through this gateway we need to make ourselves lighter once more, let go of the more weighty concerns of the earth element. It is time to gain a more spatially aware perspective, and consider the views of another. Ask yourself: *Who are you to me and who am I, seen through your eyes?*

The heart and the feather

In the calendar, we have reached an important turning point in the year, the Autumn Equinox, which occurs on 22 or 23 September. For the second time in the annual round, the hours of daytime and night-time are equalised. The Sun rises due east and sets due west across the whole planet and a near-perfect equilibrium of light and dark is experienced. The symbol of this balance is a set of scales, the only mechanical zodiac image, and here we draw back from our instincts towards a more considered, more dispassionate spirit of enquiry. The name Libra draws its root from the name of a Libyan goddess of justice who carried scales of judgement.[1] In Egypt, she was known as Ma'at, who maintained a spirit of truth, fairness and justice. Egyptian books of the dead, maps of the afterlife which are consistently found on scrolls interred with the deceased, depict a scene where a person's heart is being weighed against a single feather in the scales of Ma'at. She is both the feather and the scales and holds the balance necessary to preserve the natural order, ensuring that only those whose heart has achieved balance may pass into the Field of Reeds, the blissful afterlife. For those of heavy heart, the soul is devoured by a crocodile-headed demon. In the agricultural cycle, this is when the crop is weighed and an assessment made on the success or failure of the year's harvest. If the right rituals have been conducted and the gods are in accordance, the community can pass into the winter months secure in the knowledge that their need for nourishment will be met. If not, the scales record an imbalance and the community suffers, unless compensations are put in place. The scales themselves, though, remain impartial.

Harmony and proportion

This ideal of Libran impartiality is emphasised through the blindfolded Greek goddess Themis, a prophetess and personification of the social order of law and customs on Mount Olympus. She 'unites the gods in assemblies, and does the same for human beings'.[2] Often conflated with the Roman goddess Justitia, she has scales and a sword, in the same manner as St Michael the Archangel. In the Christian calendar, the feast of Michaelmas is celebrated in late September while the Sun is in Libra.[3] The blindfolded aspect of Themis enables her to see within, beyond the manifestations of life. Being unable to see outwardly, she is freed from the distractions of the dominant visual sense that is so easily seduced by external forms and so susceptible to partiality and prejudice. This is a paradox, as Librans tend to be especially sensitive to appearances, the way things look; they like things to match! Venus rules Libra and she finds her sense of proportion in this sign, her beauty expressed as a harmony, things being in right relationship, tending towards an ideal of perfect balance that might transcend the unstable flux of the material world.

The mystery of attraction

This is the second of the air signs in the wheel and, once again, as in Gemini, we bring attention to our breath, focusing now on the balance of inhalation and exhalation, aware of how our thoughts lead us this way and that. We notice the quality of our relating, and how our ideas are inspired, influenced and modified through our social encounters. Libra medicine points to the mystery of attraction and the realisation that the people we are attracted to – whether as lovers, spouses, business partners or opponents – carry a critical part of our own soul, often one that we are less aware of, or are unwilling to fully claim as our own. While there is truth in the old adage *opposites attract*, often we are drawn to someone because we have not learned to fully inhabit a particular way of being, one that our significant other may carry for us. Libra is a cardinal sign that bestows upon the air element a directive quality, made manifest through the initiative of the relationship encounter, the dynamic meeting of self and other, born of an impulse to find harmony. The Taoist concept of yin and yang embodies this dynamic dance of opposites: light and dark, male and female, active and receptive energy. The beauty of this interplay of dualities lies at the heart of this sign.

Opposition invites relationship

Libra marks the first time that we meet a sign energy that directly opposes one that we have already encountered. In terms of the calendar, we are six months in, halfway around the wheel; for the first time we stare, face to face, into the eyes of our opposite number. Libra's opposite sign, Aries, is full of single-minded impulse and warrior-like passion. Libra seeks to temper the excesses of such desires with a spirit of consideration and reflection, mediation and refinement, fairness and reconciliation. Libra actively directs our attention away from individual egoic expression towards the possibility of relationship. The Arien impulse *I Am* has transformed into *We Are*; it is nothing less than a declaration of interdependence. This is the first time on our journey where we are forced to consider the consequences of our actions on others and see things from another's perspective. Through Libra we can become conscious of the play of opposites within ourselves and how this tension manifests itself in the world through love and conflict. Consider the following quote by C.G. Jung:

The psychological rule says that when an inner situation is not made conscious, it happens outside as fate. That is to say, when the individual remains undivided and does not become conscious of his inner opposite, the world must perforce act out the conflict and be torn into opposing halves.[4]

The blind prophet

In this context, consider the story of Tiresias, who receives an unusual, and remarkably Libran, gift of trans-sexual initiation from Hera.[5] He is permitted to witness two snakes coupling in her sacred grove, after which he is granted the opportunity to experience life as a woman for a span of seven years before being transformed back into a man. He is thus given a direct way of understanding the different needs and perspectives of the two sexes, and a unique insight into the fundamental source of passion and conflict. This is all done in order to settle a bet between Hera and her husband Zeus, who quarrel over whether man or woman experiences the most pleasure from sexual union. When summoned before them to answer this question, Tiresias is in accord with Zeus's own belief that woman experiences the greater pleasure, asserting that she enjoys nine-tenths of it, and man only one-tenth. Hera is enraged at this hitherto secret information being exposed and she immediately blinds Tiresias. Zeus, though, pleased to be vindicated, grants him the gift of prophecy, and so this blind man becomes the most famous seer of the ancient world, consulted by heroes and warriors before many an important quest or battle. His blindness and his knowledge of polarity open his inner eye.

The art of suspending judgement

We could justifiably substitute the idea of prophecy for that of wise judgement, the ability to hold in awareness both sides of an opposition without being swayed one way or the other. This was the contemplative practice of the ancient Greek Skeptics who doubted, or abstained from believing in, the validity of any claim to the absolute truth of how to acquire knowledge about the world. This is somewhat different from the way the word 'sceptic' is used today; the ancient Skeptics were opposed to all forms of dogmatism and employed a practice of *epoche* – suspending judgement – to attain a state of *ataraxia*, or tranquillity of mind.[6] This is an example of a philosophy practised as an art of living, a middle path that acknowledges the tension, polarity and opposition inherent within the human experience, life and the cosmos, and attempts to hold the balance between opposing forces.

A Libran practice for dealing with conflict

One of Libra's key roles in the zodiac is to take the excess heat out of tense situations. We can do this by simply noticing where we carry an especially passionate charge in ourselves and where it shows up in our relationships. Stepping into another person's shoes, practising seeing things from their perspective, is good Libran medicine. However unreasonable another person's behaviour might seem to you, from their perspective it makes sense, and your actions probably seem unreasonable to them. Understanding can only happen when we let go of the need to be right. If you are faced with a conflict, imagine a pair of scales, with each of your grievances, complaints and judgements holding weight on either side in each of the two pans. See the pans rocking to either side, and if you can, shift from your point of view between the two perspectives and spend time seeing it from the other viewpoint, before positioning your awareness in the centre, remaining conscious of the tensions pulling on either side and without being drawn by either.

To take this a stage further, we can actively reach out in appreciation of the significant others in our lives. When we can hold that balance point within ourselves, we are better able to comprehend the way others mirror back to us exactly what we need in order to achieve wholeness. Let someone close to you know much they mean to you, tell them what a difference they make and have made in your life, and how much you appreciate that. Start with the easier relationships; then perhaps move on to harder ones. Consider this extract from a poem by Rumi:

Out beyond ideas of wrong-doing
And right-doing

There is a field.
I'll meet you there.
When the soul lies down in that grass
the world is too full to talk about.[7]

Catching the colours as they turn

If a year were a day, the Autumn Equinox would be the sunset,
and this is the best time of day to connect with the spirit of
this sign. The Arien dawn beckons us to awaken from our
night-time slumber and anticipate the day ahead; sunset, by
contrast, tends to relax our ambitions, reminding us of the
need to let go of outer concerns, to rest and reflect. Autumn
leaves, in the process of their
dying, entice us first with
their beauty as their colours
turn golden, red and orange.
The colours of dusk constellate our imaginings and turn

our minds towards the beauty of union before darkness falls.
We are enthralled, but at the same time conscious of what that
beauty means. It inspires the artist in us, trying to catch the
colours as they turn. Seducing our imaginations, Libra is the
sweetly packaged usherette of darkness, the true impact of
which will be confronted in the next sign, Scorpio. We are
being initiated into an expanded awareness of who we are
through a process of contemplation on the nature of opposition and its irresistible attraction.

The wedding of opposites

Libra presents us with a wedding of light and shadow, and with it a ceremony, so beautifully designed, choreographed to produce an archetypal image of togetherness. The longing we all have to unite with one another will draw us into a marriage that will require us to give up our individual status, to merge our own unique light with that of our chosen opposite. But we are only flirting with commitment in Libra, dancing with it, as we idealistically attempt to tailor agreements and contracts to meet the unforeseen challenges that may lie ahead. We are seeing the world through rose-tinted glasses, yet at the same time donning the blindfold of Themis. In finding union with another, we are marking the end of a life chapter when we only had to think about ourselves. What lies beyond that threshold necessarily remains unknown.

The beauty contest: Libran shadow energy

It was at one of the great wedding ceremonies of Greek myth, that of the river goddess Thetis and the mortal Peleus, where the Libran shadow revealed itself most tellingly. The wedding was celebrated on Mount Pelion, outside Chiron's cave, with all twelve Olympian deities in attendance, seated on twelve thrones. Things began well; blessings were bestowed, rites offered in their proper place, and the divine guests were getting along just fine. However, weddings have been known to turn sour and so it was on this occasion, for one goddess had been strategically omitted from the guest list: Eris (Roman, Discordia). Not inviting discord to a wedding is understandable but a high price was paid for this omission. Eris gatecrashed the ceremony and, determined to put the divine guests at loggerheads, placed a golden apple before the three great goddesses, Hera, Athena and Aphrodite, bearing the inscription 'To the Fairest'. Each stepped forward to claim it, and the gods dared not judge it. So Paris, the young, ambitious prince of Troy (with outstanding Libran good looks), was invited to settle the question. Thus ensued the most famous of all beauty contests. Each goddess in turn presented herself and offered Paris a tempting bribe. Hera offered a powerful marriage that would bring glory to his kingdom; Athena, military aid that would more or less guarantee him victory in war. Then up stepped Aphrodite, goddess of love; she simply dropped her tunic, bedazzling the young prince with her beauty, and offered him the hand of the most beautiful woman in the world, Helen of Sparta. Paris, of course, was too vain and too much the lover to refuse such an offer. Aphrodite won the contest and Paris wooed Helen away from her Spartan husband Menelaus, sparking the greatest war in ancient history, at Troy. Helen, thereafter, became known as the face that launched a thousand ships.[8] Venus is forever chained to Mars, the god of war, her eternal lover, just as Libra is always tied to its opposite sign, Aries. The whole saga of the beauty contest upset the natural and social order in the greatest way possible, and when Themis – justice – is offended, Nemesis – retribution – appears.[9]

The uninvited guest

Not inviting Eris to the wedding is the Libran shadow energy, and it is no coincidence that she bears the same forbidden fruit for which Eve was banished from the Garden. Eris is that aspect of the feminine that we cannot see, the dark aspect whose exclusion within patriarchal culture lies at the heart of a woman's resentment. When the true beauty of the feminine is rejected and denied any appreciation of its depth, life becomes a vain contest for attention and appreciation. Woman struggles to stay fully in her power, and is more likely to succumb to man's uninitiated, lustful urge for instant gratification. She fails to inspire him to undertake the rites of initiation for which he unconsciously longs. Until he does, he cannot be trusted to truly care for her, and can never truly know her. Only when Eris is invited can the deeper conflicts between man and woman be addressed. Confronting the repressed aspects of the female psyche can be deeply uncomfortable, but it encourages trust and opens up the possibility of a more profound understanding. Yes, of course we want everything to be beautiful at the wedding feast, for there to be harmony. We want things to be in accord, we want everyone to get along, for it to be a perfect day. But in that quest for perfection there is almost certainly someone missing from the party. When the priest asks: 'Is there anyone here who knows of any just cause why these two people should not be wed in holy matrimony?' there is a moment when all present hold their breath, just in case the uninvited guest shows up after all.

Too much or too little Libra

Being too reliant on the Libran perspective, you may be overconcerned with how you come across to others, too focused in the other and not rooted enough in yourself. Sometimes we try so hard to overaccommodate another that we betray our own integrity, brushing things under the carpet in order to make everything look all right. We try to put everything in a positive light, and it is hard to fully trust someone who does this. There is also a fine line between suspending judgement, which is an art of enquiry, and vacillation, which is the avoidance of difficult issues and decisions. It might take a generous dose of Aries medicine to help make you more decisive and self-willed. If you have too little representation in this sign, or a lack of access to the air element in general, you might find it hard to appreciate other people's views and ways of doing things. Taking on this medicine by becoming more considered in the way you think and act will help restore your integrity in this perspective. There may be a need to get things in proportion, take a step back from everyday concerns, rest and reflect. Perhaps spend more time contemplating the beauty around you, the harmony in nature and the cosmos.

The Dance of Venus

To conclude this chapter, I will share one of the most beautiful examples of cosmic harmony that I know of, the so-called Dance of Venus, as a contemplative image for Libra. Every eight years, Earth's sister planet and ruler of Libra draws a

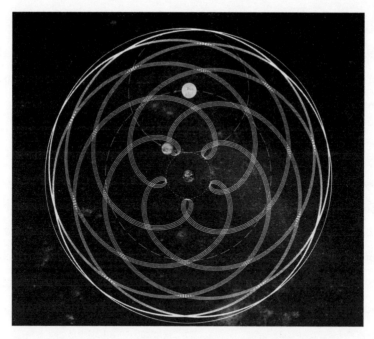

The Dance of Venus: Image courtesy of John Martineau /
Wooden Books

beautiful five-petalled rose pattern in space around us. This
remarkable dance is composed of five heart-shaped movements,
each consisting of an inferior and superior conjunction to the
Sun,[10] which themselves form two perfect pentagrams in the
zodiac over the eight years. The rose and the pentagram are
traditional symbols of Venus, as is the apple, which reveals a
pentagram in its five-pipped core when cut in half. Eight
Earth years equates to exactly thirteen Venus years; the difference between these numbers produces the five petals of the
rose pattern. Five, eight and thirteen are numbers widely used
in the flowering patterns of plants, and are the early numbers
in the Fibonacci sequence, which approximates to the Golden
Mean, a ratio which produces perfect harmony and is itself

embodied in the pentagram.[11] The extraordinary beauty and coherence within this great 'cosmic coincidence' may astound our rational minds, while stirring our souls to a deeper realisation, the maxim of Libra: *Truth is Beauty and Beauty, Truth.*

Libra summary

Spend time during this seventh stage of the wheel contemplating the nature of relationship, the nature of opposition and your connection with beauty as truth. Engage with the following enquiries and suggested activities.

CONSIDER THESE QUESTIONS, ASK YOURSELF:

- What am I balancing in my life at the moment?

- In what ways could I step back from a challenging situation, suspend judgement of it and simply observe it from a place of non-attachment?

- Where am I not being fully honest in a relationship and in what ways am I trying to keep up appearances?

- Which part of myself have I banished from the wedding feast? What is at risk if I invite that part to the table?

SUGGESTED PRACTICES AND ACTIVITIES

Think about a 'significant other' in your life. This might be a partner, lover, ex-partner/ex-lover, family member or opponent. Choose someone with whom you have a significant emotional charge, whether positive or negative. Then consider:

- What attracted you to this person?

- What emotional charge do you hold for this person?

- In what way is this person holding up a mirror for you? What might this person reflect back to you about yourself?

- What do you love and/or appreciate about this person?

A CONTEMPLATION OF BEAUTY

Part One: Think about these questions:

- What does beauty mean to you?

- Think of someone in your life, or a place, or a work of art that you find really beautiful. What qualities does this person or object have that enable you to appreciate this beauty?

- What qualities can you identify *in yourself* that enable you to appreciate this beauty?

Part Two: Take yourself to a place of natural and/or aesthetic/ artistic beauty: a natural environment that really speaks to you – an art gallery or a building of great beauty. Just allow yourself to become immersed in that beauty, become one with it, let it envelop you.

The Eighth Gateway

Scorpio

Sun in Scorpio period: *22/23 October – 21/22 November*

Symbol: *The Scorpion/Eagle*

Motivation: *Fixed/establishing and maintaining*

Element (temperament): *Water*

Ruling planets: *Mars and Pluto*

Body parts ruled: *Genitals, bowels*

Keynote: *I commit. I surrender the light.*

Version of the truth: *Does it go deep enough? Can it bear its own death and transformation?*

Medicine: *Deep soul connection. Facing the shadow.*

Shadow energy: *Self-sabotage. Treachery. Vengefulness.*

Mantra: *I face my own shadow, and in so doing, I honour the depth of my soul.*

The transition from Libra to Scorpio

That rather unsettling line in the wedding ceremony, 'til death do us part', shows us a way into this transition. Within the idealism of the Libran union the romantic notion of eternal togetherness has us spellbound. But as the curtain of night falls and autumn's chilling sting is felt, the deeper consequences of the commitment take hold. The exquisite poise of the Libran equinox is short-lived; night soon overtakes day and the life force of nature withdraws. The turning leaves, whose rich colours so enchanted us, are fallen and are being digested by all manner of tiny life forms, rotting them down into the dark, damp earth. We must surrender the aesthetic balance, with its proportionate beauty, as we enter this composting phase of the wheel, face what it is in ourselves that is rotten or rotting, and embrace it; in time this will become the soil that breeds new life and opportunity. Scorpio compels us to look inward, with her moody skies, fading light and autumn evenings drawing in around us like a dark cloak. We have reason to mistrust the vitality of what we see around us during this phase and must allow certain aspects of our lives to die, while staying mindful and being prepared to grieve the loss.

Penetrating the deeper truth

To seek balance in all things is one of the noblest aims in life. It is the breeding ground of a happy and contented existence. In order for this to be authentic, however, we must strive to achieve a true balance within ourselves and often we settle for a more superficial equilibrium. This might look well adjusted on the surface, but it so often fails to address the deeper truth of our soul's journey. Have a look at the compromises you have made in your life. What deals and agreements have you made with others, and yourself, in order to keep the peace, to avoid conflict, or to keep up appearances? Notice how they sit with you right now. What aspects of yourself have you had to deny in order to keep your life in a seeming balance? And to what extent are you willing to risk upsetting the harmony in order to penetrate the more truthful, uncomfortable layers of your being? To do that, we must deal with the intensity of our feelings, the proximity of pain, the merging of our psychic energies, the destructive patterns we meet in others. Our unprocessed fears, jealousies and karmic debts are being mirrored back to us by our spouses and lovers, who will carry this psychic material until we are ready to own it ourselves. The truest commitment that you can make now is to know the contents of your shadow, for while you are busy building up a heroic image of yourself, the shadow walks beside you and, in the words of Antonio Machado, it 'tends to be what you are not'.[1] Your shadow is not your enemy, it preserves for you a wealth of hidden resources, if you would but acknowledge them. As you enter the gateway of Scorpio, ask yourself: *Where have I buried my treasure?*

The seeds of life sown under the ground

Remembering Scorpio's opposite sign, the greening, blossoming sign of Taurus, the contrast is stark. The zodiac is a wheel of change and offers a great teaching about opposite-complementary forces. Mars-ruled Scorpio opposes Venus-ruled Taurus, just as it follows Venus-ruled Libra. Mars carries a sexual charge which we met in fertile Aries, with its spring-time enthusiasm driving life outwards and upwards, through the doorway of birth. In Scorpio that potency is driven inwards and downwards, and for the sake of life's continuity the seeds of life must return to the black earth; for the sake of true human understanding they must penetrate the dark recesses of the soul. This is the doorway of death that leads to rebirth. Birth and death are portals within the larger cycle of life, and Scorpio medicine is the acceptance that our time-limited bodies will wither and decay, along with the personality that attaches itself to the physical form. In the glyph for Scorpio we see a symbol which appears as an 'M', the right-hand stem of which turns into an arrow, which drops down below the rest of the symbol. In a similar way, the tail of the Scorpius constellation plunges well below the ecliptic path, and always remains hidden in the northernmost latitudes.[2] This tail is both the death sting of the Scorpion and the potent seed that Mother Nature secretes at this time of the year. It is sown under the ground, carrying the latent energy of regeneration within it, the life force being quietly preserved, hidden from view, throughout the winter months.

M for Magdalene

Staying with the glyph, let us consider the 'M' of the symbol. We encountered it in Virgo, associated with the Virgin Mary, and rites of purification.[3] In Scorpio, the 'M' is more likely to symbolise Mary Magdalene and rites of sexual initiation. Denigrated in orthodox Christian theology and twisted into the image of the 'fallen woman', she nonetheless holds a critical role in the Christian story, being the first person to greet the risen Christ and the only witness to his resurrection. Margaret Starbird identifies Magdalene as *initiatrix*,[4] drawing upon evidence from the Gnostic gospels (found at Nag Hammadi in the 1940s), suggesting that she was his closest companion and, indeed, the one who initiated him into the mysteries of love and death and renewal.[5] Patriarchal religions have long sought to control and subdue the sexual potency of the feminine, so the image of Magdalene has been tarnished. Like female figures of power before her, such as Eve, Lilith and Eris, she has been cast into the mythological shadow. By denying the restorative power of the feminine, the crucial relationship that human beings have with their sexual energy and with the transformative power of nature is lost. Everything that is hidden from view is experienced as a threat. This leaves woman destabilised in her core and liable to emotional manipulation, while man becomes disengaged from his own creative energy, seeking ever more to control, objectify and procure her many gifts. The power of Magdalene is ever-present, though, and if we can restore the integrity of her image in the psyche and let her administer the elixir that she carries in her famous alabaster jar, a journey of deep healing and regeneration awaits us.

The scorpion of the west

A giant scorpion was sent by Gaia, the earth goddess, to inflict a poisonous sting upon the boastful hunter, Orion, who had threatened to slay all the beasts of the Earth.[6] As the constellation of Scorpius rises in the east, Orion is seen to fall below the western horizon; the two opponents are never seen in the sky at the same time. Orion's stars were known to the Egyptians as Osiris. This god of resurrection and growth was also dispatched to the Underworld by a scorpion's sting (in some variants of his myth) to be reborn as falcon-headed Horus.[7] This is sometimes likened to the transformation of the scorpion into the eagle, considered by some to be a *higher* expression of this sign.[8] The Scorpius constellation has a powerful red star at its heart, Antares, the Watcher of the West, one of the four royal stars which would have been aligned to the cardinal points in ancient times.[9] For the Egyptians it marked the gateway into the land of the dead, which was always oriented to the west, being the direction in which the Sun and all stellar bodies set beneath the horizon. In Egypt, royal burial was always conducted on the west side of the Nile, as with the pyramids at Giza and the Valley of the Kings at Thebes (modern Luxor).

The poppy

When British veterans returned to the fields of Flanders the year after the end of the First World War, they saw fields of red poppies where the bodies of their fellow soldiers had fallen, and this sight is said to have reminded them of the blood that had been spilt there. The poppy was then instituted as the symbol of remembrance and it has been traditional in Britain to wear one in your buttonhole in the first weeks of November each year, to remember those who gave their lives. Traditionally, early November is the time to honour the ancestors; the Celtic festival of Samhain, All Hallow's Eve (Halloween), the Day of the Dead all mark a liminal time of year when the boundary between this world and the otherworld is said to be at its thinnest and can be most easily crossed. This coincides with the time of year when initiation rites are conducted in certain traditions, in which poppies sometimes feature. As a flower of the Underworld, the poppy evokes both sleep and death; Hypnos (Somnus) and Thanatos (Mors), the two sons of Night, both have poppies closely associated with them. At the entrance of the cave they inhabit these shadowy figures beckon the sleeper in, fingers pressed against pursed lips, shaking bunches of poppies in their hands and offering a goblet of their juice. Poppies produce opium, the drug of choice for the soul-seeking romantic poets, and archaeological finds at ancient burial sites confirm that the poppy was used as a sacred plant in Underworld rites of passage.[10] Demeter, grieving the loss of her beloved daughter Persephone, sought relief from her pain by ingesting the flower.[11]

The descent of Persephone

Poppies make us think of blood, with their bright crimson colouring, of menstrual blood, of the blood of initiation, the blood shed in childbirth. The black core of the flower reminds us of death, and this combination puts us in mind of the two rulers of this sign: blood-red Mars and black-as-night Pluto. Greek Hades lures Persephone with a poppy (in one variant of the myth) abducting her into his realm, and later persuading her to eat of the pomegranate, which oozes with blood-red juice. This ties her to the Underworld, and thereafter she becomes its queen. We are told that Hades tricked her on both occasions; but Persephone's apparently innocent curiosity was surely the inevitable longing of her soul to be initiated. She is drawn across the threshold from childhood into womanhood, through the crimson promise of knowl- edge and experience; to know the secrets of her own sexual nature and the mystery of death and rebirth. Each year, at her autumnal descent, she returns below ground to become the mistress and secret-keeper of all that lies hidden, while above ground her mother's withdrawal into grief foreshadows winter's sleep.

The soul's desire for truth

The maternal cohesion we felt in the first water sign, Cancer, is broken in Scorpio; with the severing of the bond between mother and child a crisis of abundance ensues. Sometimes life's circumstances will bring us to our knees and we will feel powerless to do anything about them. This could occur through illness, injury or the death of a loved one, but it could also manifest as an inner compulsion to jeopardise one's own security: making a reckless business decision, going deeply into debt, getting involved with a dangerous lover. Such actions may appear to all the world like self-sabotage, but are actually part of the death urge arising from deep within the soul which compels us to journey downwards into the shadowlands. It is really a deep desire for truth, authenticity and transformation. We will tend to sabotage our security in situations where we have been pretending that everything is all right, when really it isn't. It may account for why someone in mid-life will have an affair that threatens an apparently stable marriage. Wherever we have overcompromised for the sake of material security (Taurus) or society's approval (Libra), suppressed our deepest desires or become impotent around our sexual power, our soul will seek rebellion through Scorpio medicine.

Dark luminescence

In Western culture we rely a great deal upon our eyes and draw our metaphors for understanding from our dominant visual sense. We say things like: *I see what you mean; that's clear; thank you for enlightening me.* We assume that to become knowledge-able we must bring things into the light. While we are right to honour the Sun as the source of light and our primary metaphor for consciousness, the roots of both Eastern and Western philosophy concur that the Sun's true home is the Underworld; it rises from it each morning, and returns at the end of each day. The heroes who journey there – Odysseus, Aeneas, Parmenides – all come back with this profoundly altered understanding of the so-called Midnight Sun.[12] In alchemy the image of the black sun, *sol niger*, shines with 'a dark luminescence' that illuminates the deep mysteries of the psyche.[13] There are preparatory stages necessary before descending into Hades realm. Without preparation, without a genuine intention, without appropriate purification rites, the journey is too dangerous; the fragile human ego, so reliant on daylight, will misunderstand and fail to respect everything it encounters there.

Fire and water

Hades' realm is a place of tremendous paradox, a place where fire and water meet, as in the astrological Pluto. Scorpio is a water sign, traditionally ruled by fiery Mars, and is like liquid fire, magma moving slowly in the mantle of the earth. Rising slowly to the surface, it will erupt as volcanic lava and ash; lava destroys and, over time, will refertilise the ground of our being, and ash preserves the memory of what has gone before. The mystery school cults of ancient Greece often based themselves close to active volcanoes, precisely because it connected them to the liquid fire of the Underworld, which they understood to be purifying for the soul.[14] This journey down into the depths to a place where all the opposites meet, where you may be stripped of your dignity and status, even of your ambition to ascend, takes tremendous courage. We need experienced guides to take us there and bring us back. Those who understand its terrain and can act as caretakers know that the fiery stripping away of false personas, while painful, is delivered with the healing balm of compassion.

Scorpio medicine: eating the shadow

In order to live in truth, Scorpio teaches us that we must meet and own the shadow part of our nature. Poet Robert Bly developed Jung's concept of the shadow, comparing it to a long bag that we drag around with us and into which, during our youth, we have stuffed all the things we couldn't face about ourselves in the process of becoming 'civilised'. For a man this is likely to be his wildness, his anger, his spontaneity, his sexuality, his freedom, along with his feminine side, his *anima,* which includes both the gentle lover and the wild banshee. For a woman, her *animus,* as masculine hero and tyrant, is most likely in the bag, along with her goddess and her witch.

As adults trying to find ourselves, we want to restore an authentic relationship with these archetypes, and we are desperate to get them out of the bag. But first we must face their justifiable anger, their resentment at having been banished in the first place, and subsequently projected onto our spouses, our lovers, our children, our teachers, our communities. In those projections, we have given away energies that rightfully belong in our own treasury. In Taurus we filled our bellies and feasted on life's bounty; now, as Bly puts it, we must 'eat the shadow'.[15] We can do this through grieving our losses, through rituals and vision quests, through art and artful conversation, through depth of study, through therapy, through learning the language of soul. We need to take time out from the daily pretence of having to look good, and start claiming back those supposedly unacceptable parts of us. The shadow walks with us all of our lives; if we do not face it, it will control us, and we will live in constant fear of it and project it out onto the world at large.

We did not come to remain whole

Beyond our fear of death lies the seat of our power and the very core of desire. Scorpio is a medicine of power, of regeneration, rebirth, sexual liberation and deep healing. Far from attempting to control nature and bend it to human will, the alchemist learns to submit himself to nature's power and mystery and be digested by it. In order for the soul to thrive, we must be prepared to face our own demise, to travel the road of death while still alive, to die before we die. Bly insists that we did not come to this earth to *remain* whole, but to be broken down so that we might become whole again, to let our leaves fall, to allow what is rotten in us to decompose like the decaying organic matter of late autumn. Returning to the dark alchemical soil of our being, we might begin again 'drawing up on great roots'.[16]

The destructive side of the Scorpio shadow

Because Scorpio offers us shadow as a medicine we have focused on the shadow's healing, regenerative aspect, but we must be ever-mindful of its destructive side. Living so close to the edge, the scorpion has an extraordinary survival instinct; their natural suspicion of others' motivations and preparedness for things to turn sour renders them more ready than most to make a situation work to their advantage, often ruthlessly so. Scorpios expect the rug to be pulled from under them at any moment and are equipped to deal with that. To make sure that they don't lose out, they stay ahead of the game and they know how to make a little go a long way.

Scorpions can survive in the harshest of conditions. They can smell danger, falsehood or inauthenticity from a mile away, are capable of exploiting that as a weakness, and will precipitate another's downfall if necessary. But it so often works against them and they will tend to bring about their own undoing in the process. There is something in the Scorpio nature that tends towards ruthlessness, cruelty, self-destruction, jealousy, sabotage (often self-sabotage), sexual manipulation, revenge and psychic possession. If you are overendowed with Scorpio medicine you may need to stay especially mindful to when and how these traits arise within you; be gentle, have compassion for yourself when they do. If you are lacking in this energy, you may need to recognise where you have idealised your own inherent goodness and rightness, while projecting the destructive side of your shadow onto all those others that you have demonised in some way, and set about claiming back that side.

Wearing the hooded cloak

Every year on the Scorpio stage of *The Alchemical Journey* we invite participants to put on a black hooded cloak and contemplate the nature of their own shadow material. We make it clear that they can do this in silence, while allowing themselves to be witnessed in that place. We let each person stay there for as long as they need to. If someone chooses to share a deep hurt or confess something, the space is there for them to do that, and that can sometimes be the cathartic experience that they need, but we do not explicitly encourage it. Our dark secrets, our impossible longings and our deep griefs are possessed of soul, they belong to the Underworld. They do not always need to be brought into the potentially shaming light of open disclosure. Having them acknowledged, welcomed and treated with compassion is often enough. It is one of the most profound exercises we do all year and, even though very little is said, a deep transformation occurs.

Scorpio summary

Spend time during this eighth stage of the wheel contemplating the nature of your shadow, your relationship to death and your commitment to truth. As part of this you could engage with the following enquiries and suggested activities. Use your journal and keep your responses to yourself for now.

CONSIDER THESE QUESTIONS, ASK YOURSELF:

- What am I most deeply committed to?

- What desires do I fail to acknowledge? What do I crave that feels shameful, that I believe must be kept hidden?

- What is my soul crying out for?

- What aspects of myself have I put onto others, what could I claim back and from whom?

- How do I feel about power?

- What secrets am I keeping from others, and maybe even from myself?

- *Women:* What is my relationship to my menstrual cycle and/or menopause as spiritual/soul work?

SUGGESTED ACTIVITIES

- You could visit the grave of a deceased loved one and/or spend time in contemplation with a photo or memento that connects you to them. If you were able to ask them three questions, what would they be? Try asking them, and be open for answers to emerge through dreams or moments of synchronicity.

- Contemplate what is composting in you at the moment. If you are reading this in the autumn, go for a walk in nature and notice the processes at work: the nights drawing in, the leaves rotting down. Feel your connection with them.

- Have a sharing conversation with someone you can go deep with, and address the issues of shadow. It is best done in the evening, by candlelight; create an atmosphere that will allow you both to dig into some of the more uncomfortable areas of your lives. Notice the language you use, listen with compassion, share the depth of you.

The Ninth Gateway

Sagittarius

Sun in Sagittarius period: *21/22 November – 21/22 December*

Symbol: *The Centaur-Archer*

Motivation: *Mutable/adapting and transforming*

Element (temperament): *Fire*

Ruling planets: *Jupiter*

Body parts ruled: *Hips, thighs*

Keynote: *I journey. I experience. I know.*

Version of the truth: *Will it expand my mind? Is it far-reaching enough?*

Medicine: *Travel. Metaphysical study. Faith. Joy.*

Shadow energy: *Getting carried away. Overshooting the mark. Fundamentalist beliefs.*

Mantra: *I know the way, I am guided by the stars, and I trust that my aim is true.*

The transition from Scorpio to Sagittarius

From the shadowy depths of the soul we now rise with the spirit, like the phoenix from the ashes, into the possibility and reconception of new life. The shift into Sagittarius is a leap of faith and a leap in the dark, for this fiery impulse occurs at a time of year when we are plunging further into winter's night. This period of the Sun's journey will take us right up to the Winter Solstice on 21 December. Having passed through the doorway of death, the life force is reconceived, metaphysically freed from the confines of embodiment. By the time the Sun enters Sagittarius, the rate of acceleration by which the nights grow longer is decreasing; plotted on a graph, we would see a curve gradually bottoming out as the much-anticipated solstice approaches. This can be sensed inwardly and likened to the rekindling of an inner, spiritual, visionary fire, a fire of recovery and renewal. In Sagittarius, our soul anticipates the return of the light and an alchemical awakening occurs that predicts the regeneration and continuation of the life cycle.

What gives your life meaning?

We cannot authentically rise again until we have faced our shadow, honoured our dead and confronted the deepest longings of the soul, but we should not slumber longer than we need to in the watery realms. We are about to pass through the gateway of Sagittarius and there is a powerful calling now to come back. We are on a journey towards wholeness here, and it is important that we don't abandon ourselves completely to the Underworld descent, for it is a bottomless place that will suck the hope out of us if we let it. This next phase can uplift and reinspire you with a more expanded possibility of who you are.

Think of a time when you came back to life, when hope was restored, when you could see light again after a dark passage, when you found faith in something greater than yourself. Beyond all the fear and haunting doubt, beyond the heartbreak and suffering of loss, what is it that gives your life meaning? As you survey the furthest horizon of your life, what do you imagine could lie beyond it? Take yourself out into the wild places of nature and feel the immense majesty of creation; as night falls, spend some time under the dark, velvety sky and behold its magnificent tapestry of stars. As the wheel turns again now, allow the awe and wonder of the Universe to inspire you, and ask yourself: *What could my life be?*

The third fire sign

Sagittarius is the third of the fire signs, and taken as a trio we see an illuminating progression. The cardinal directive of Aries generates the spark that initiates life in spring; the fixed summer sign of Leo, with its royal stamp of authenticity, tends the fire, ensuring that the ever-present life force endures; Sagittarius now spreads the fire

and gives it direction. As the mutable representative of this element group, it reimagines the fiery force as both an outward adventure and an inward, philosophical or religious quest. Within the soil at this time of year, elements are recombining to warm and protect the seeds of life underground, as a new cycle of gestation begins.

Looking to the stars

The medicine of Sagittarius is freedom: freedom to think a new thought, dream a new dream, imagine a different future. This stage of the wheel has the potential to reopen your heart and release the highest calling of your spirit. Our minds now stretch towards higher ideals, an image of who we might be beyond our physical nature. The Sagittarian archer takes aim and looses his arrow towards the far horizon. We might naturally look to the stars for guidance, for a sign, just as three wise astrologers did when they followed a star in the East that led them to a stable in Bethlehem. This is the season of Advent; Christians anticipate the birth of Christ, just as pagans look forward to the rebirth of the Sun at Winter Solstice.

By Jove!

We associate Sagittarius with benevolence, far-sightedness and a breadth of understanding, and this sign is ruled by Jupiter, the largest planet of the solar system, a giant ball of gas that dwarfs our own planet, and one of the brightest planets we can see in our night skies. Larger-than-life Jupiter (Greek Zeus), the most powerful of the gods on Mount Olympus, is known for his magnanimity and expansive vision, as a progenitor and protector of humanity, a bestower of good fortune. The planet that carries his name has long performed a benevolent role for the Earth. Due to its colossal size and gravitational pull, it draws a multitude of comets and meteors into its orbit, protecting us from cosmic debris that might otherwise be destined for Earth.[1] He can also be a fearsome god who brings fire upon the Earth. With thunderbolt in hand, it is he 'who shak'st with fiery light the World'.[2]

The trained eye of the archer

The Sagittarian 'feelgood' factor reflects the constellation image of Chiron, the wise and kindly centaur, and mentor to the heroes of Greek myth.[3] This has been established since Greek times, but it was not the original attribution. Sagittarius is an archer, and the centaur's arrow is usually depicted pointing skywards, as befits one whose message is to inspire the spirit towards liberation. But an archer, of course, is also a sniper, a killer, and this description better fits the pre-Greek tradition. For the Egyptians this constellation was depicted more simply as a hand holding an arrow. The ancient cunei-form tablets refer to the figure as god of war, whose primary motivation was martial, rather than educational. It is not until the Classical era that the constellation develops into the part-animal figure we are more familiar with today; not a centaur at first, but a two-legged satyr (half-man, half-goat) called Crotus. He became cultured and wise, unlike his fellow satyrs, but was also a skilled hunter, and is said to have invented the bow.[4]

The flaming arrow that flies from the archer's bow carries an uncompromising, warrior-like intention and focus. In stark contrast to the Gemini twins, who forever bounce ideas back and forth, the Sagittarian eye is trained on one big idea and will pursue it with passionate intent. Our modern under-standing of Sagittarius affords the archer the capacity to rise beyond his warrior instinct, directing his singular aim towards the heavens, towards God, and as such this becomes a medicine of redemption, faith and philosophy. This dichotomy contains within it a developmental theme from instinct to intellect, one to which we will return.

Wild horse medicine

Accepting Sagittarius as a centaur, we are dealing with the energy of a horse, which holds a particularly sacred place in the human imagination. Horses are at once feral, vital and raw; yet at the same time we humans have learned to 'break' horses, attempting to train that wildness out of them. A wild horse conjures up images of free sexual expression, ecstatic movement and instinctual power, while a horse that has been trained and brought under control appears cultured and disciplined, a servant and companion to humans. Horses are symbols of fertility and rebirth, sexual healing and harvest. To the Celts, the horse was an earthly manifestation of the goddess and was venerated by the Romans as Epona (from which we derive the word 'pony').[5] Images of her were hewn out of the chalk on the prominent hillsides of the North Wessex Downs in England and her feast day in the Roman calendar fell during the month of Sagittarius. The horse is depicted in some cultures as a bridge between manifest and unmanifest reality, a psychopomp that can travel between the worlds, an agent of spirit flight.[6]

Chiron: mentor to heroes

Only the body and legs of the centaur belong to the horse; the head, torso and arms are human, a fusion of wildness and civility. Chiron is sometimes referred to as the ancestor of the race of centaurs, sometimes as their priest or king.[7] In most versions of Chiron's myth, he is set apart from the other centaurs, who are notorious for their unruly behaviour, drunkenness and lechery. They were continuously at war with their more civilised neighbours, the Lapiths, who were said to have invented the bridling of horses.[8] Chiron was abandoned at birth. His divine father, Cronos, had pursued the beautiful nymph, Phyliria, who transformed herself into a mare and outran him. Cronos, though, turned himself into a stallion and took her by surprise. Chiron was born of this equine union to a father who had no interest in him and a mother so disgusted at having produced such a deformed child that she had herself turned into a linden-tree. Having been left for dead, Chiron was found and adopted by Apollo, who had a powerful civilising influence on the wild young centaur, educating him in the arts of music, archery, mathematics, rhetoric and astronomy. He grows up to become a wise mentor and guide to great heroes such as Achilles, Jason and Hercules. And it is his ever-boisterous and clumsy student Hercules who accidentally inflicts a terrible wound on Chiron from a poisoned arrow. This would have been fatal were he not immortal. In an attempt to cure his endless suffering, Chiron takes on a shamanic role as the wounded healer, eventually sacrificing his immortality in exchange for being relieved of his pain.[9] The archetypes of the mentor and the wounded healer/ shaman are expressed through Sagittarian medicine.

Dionysus and Apollo

Both satyrs and centaurs are part of the retinue of Dionysus, the lusty god of religious ecstasy and intoxication, who characterises the wilder aspects of Sagittarius. Jim Morrison, lead singer of The Doors, was born under this sign, and styled himself after Dionysus; Sagittarian William Blake wrote that 'the road of excess leads to the palace of wisdom'.[10] Chiron, by contrast, is reared in the spirit of Apollonian reason, philosophy and foresight, becoming a mentor and sage, a rather different expression of the Sagittarian desire to explore the frontiers of knowledge and experience. Peter Shaffer's play *Equus* explores the relationship between a psychiatrist with an intellectual passion for pagan animism and a young teenage patient who has a religious and sexual obsession with horses. The boy's worship of Equus has caused him, in a frenzied moment of rapture, to commit an atrocious act of blinding six horses. The intensity of the relationship between doctor and patient stirs a deep sense of unrest within the psychiatrist's mind; his reluctance to facilitate the boy's journey back to some kind of normality reflects his personal frustration at the lack of worshipful passion in his own life. He becomes envious of the boy's access to the wild, his natural ability to experience orgiastic pleasure and pain, his willingness to surrender himself to sensation. The play draws powerfully on Nietzsche's philosophical dichotomy between the Apollonian values of rationalism, education and control of instinct, in contrast to the Dionysian desire for sensuous delirium.[11] Apollo is also a god of oracles and an expert archer. He has a magical arrow of prophecy, healing and wisdom, capable of dispelling sickness and elevating the mind to lofty heights of understanding.[12] Dionysus is born from Zeus's thigh, the part of the body ruled by Sagittarius, and the arrow wound which catalyses Chiron's vocation as medicine man is to the thigh in the horse half of his body. This compels the centaur to consult the instinctual power of his animal nature in his own healing quest.

Artemis – goddess of the wild hunt

Apollo may be the acceptable face of civilised humanity, but he has a feral sister. When the twelve Olympian deities gather in assembly, Artemis (Roman Diana) takes the Sagittarian seat.[13]

She lives for the hunt and is also a great protector of animals. Choosing the freedom of the forest over romantic involvement with either men or gods, she holds her chastity sacred. Distinct from the practised withdrawal and purification rites encountered in Virgo, her virginity is fiercer, freer in its expression, wild as the natural powers with which she dances, ecstatic. She cannot be claimed or domiciled by any civilised man, as the hunter, Actaeon, learns when he makes the mistake of peering into her sacred grove and glimpses her naked there. He pays a high price for his moment of voyeuristic epiphany; Artemis turns him into a stag and he is hunted to death by his own hounds. Thereafter she wears his antlers as a totem.[14] Though uncompromising when her freedom is violated, Artemis also carries a humanitarian side. There is no limit to her compassion for those without a voice or mandate. She campaigns for what is right and just and, ferocious as she is in her desires, she also seeks a meaningful union with nature's wild pleasures.

The mystical moment of conception

We are ascending into the metaphysical heavens, launched on Apollo's arrow, with fiery intention into the far yonder. At the same time, the creative force is being rekindled in the seasonal womb of wintertime, that dark place of wisdom where the seed of life can germinate secretly beneath the ground, readying itself for Aries' springtime birth. Within A.T. Mann's life-time astrology cycle, the ninth house or Sagittarian phase of the wheel corresponds to conception and the first seven weeks of gestation.[15] This is a point of profound spiritual beginnings, which Mann describes as the entry into the transcendent octave of the zodiac. It sets a template for our later spiritual development, a pattern initiated at the moment of our conception as the male seed embeds itself in the woman's ovum. The circumstances at that moment set in motion the spiritual course of your life, determining the nature of your religious instincts and the trajectory of your aspirational pursuits. The way in which our mother first experiences the impregnation of man's creative fire will be reflected in our first creative or sexual urges, impulses that unconsciously seek to know their spiritual origins. Thus the mystery of our sexuality is forever bound with our quest for spiritual understanding, just as the instinctive, Dionysian animal part of us is forever tied to the humanising, Apollonian quest for meaning.

At full stretch

Sagittarius stretches us to the limit and beyond, and at this turning of the wheel we are called upon to extend ourselves in some way, going further than is comfortable, imagining more than we might normally believe possible. Here we experience the tension between our animal and human selves and are, in some way, forced to grow, expanding our bodies or our minds, be it sexually, religiously, philosophically or hedonistically. Sagittarius inspires us to go further *out there* and deeper *in there*, across strange foreign lands, into unchartered territories of the mind. We can experience that tension as we draw back the bow, feel the full stretch in our torso, our spine at full twist.

The Sagittarian shadow: blind faith

Sagittarius is a sign of faith. Sagittarians are often possessed of strong knowing; if you ask them how they can be so sure of something, they will probably tell you that they *just know.* This charismatic trait can lead many who are well endowed with this medicine to become teachers and guides. Sagittarians inspire others to believe, and their fiery conviction can be infectious; but when it is not grounded and made accountable, nor tempered by intellect and empathy, it can turn to dogmatism in which a person dismisses the need to enquire, check their sources, or engage in meaningful dialogue. So is born the evangelist, the missionary or the fundamentalist preacher who is convinced that there is only one answer, one way of seeing something, one route to salvation. While the experience of having total faith in something can feel extraordinarily liberating, it can also take us over and make us lose perspective.

Too much or too little Sagittarius

If we have an excess of this medicine in our charts and in our lives, we may fail to judge the size of things. Prone to exaggeration and a lack of sensitivity, Sagittarians can sometimes blow things out of proportion, or completely underestimate the impact that their tactless honesty has had on another. Sometimes, when we are overreliant on this energy, we find it harder to articulate what we mean in a way that others can understand. And when questioned about our strongly held beliefs, we might fail to convince the doubter or the sceptic because we do not really see why we should have to justify what, to us, is so evidently true! So we feel misunderstood and that fiery temperament can spark off a kind of righteous anger, alienating and disengaging others. Here we need to lean more into the ways of the opposite sign, Gemini, and learn the skills of dialogue and artful communication. These two signs complement each other, Gemini providing a constant stream of information drawn from different perspectives, which can benefit from the directional thrust and energy that Sagittarius has in abundance. Likewise, Sagittarius needs to find the words that can carry divinely inspired wisdom into the world, a voice that others will listen to within a conversation in which they feel included. If you are under-sourced in this energy you may lack the conviction to follow your dreams and to take the action that you need to bring them about. You may struggle for faith, forever doubting whether the path you are on is the right one. You may allow yourself to get knocked back too easily when things don't go your way and retreat into old habits, stories and complaints. In this case, you need to take a hearty draught of this medicine, pick up your bow and arrow and learn to wield it. Indeed, taking up archery might be just the thing; the physical act of drawing a bow and learning to loose an arrow embodies this medicine perfectly.

Focusing on your big-picture vision

You can activate this medicine in your life by imagining the big-picture vision of your life, and drawing the energy for this from the instinctual power of your horse-self. Here's something you can do: if you're able-bodied, set aside a day for a walk in nature; make it a decent distance, one where you will need to stretch yourself a little. Choose a route that will inspire you, a beautiful landscape, perhaps with some big open vistas. Take a notebook with you. Treat this walk as a meditation on the life that you are creating for yourself. Imagine, with each stride you take, that you are walking into your future, a future you have the power to imagine into reality. Maintain conscious awareness of the lower half of your body as you walk, feel into your hips and thighs. Connect with the power of the earth beneath your feet and feel it moving up through your body, feeding your mind; imagine your mind expanding. Look to the wide-open spaces around you and see your life opening out to those spaces; look to the horizon and imagine yourself travelling beyond it. Let the wings of your mind unfold and allow a vision of your future to reveal itself before you. Don't hold back on what's possible and don't reality-test it (save that for Capricorn); just allow yourself to see the possibility of who you are and what your life could be. Imagine you are free of constraints, with no limitations or conditions placed upon you. Write down what you see. When you get home, or in the days that follow, create a vision board for yourself; get a large piece of card, cut out pictures with inspiring words and affirmations to go with them and stick them on. Keep adding to it and put it up on a wall somewhere where you will see it every day. Keep imagining yourself living that life, living into those possibilities, as if it is happening now.

Sagittarius summary

Spend time during this ninth stage of the wheel looking at what really inspires you and seeing life as a journey of exploration and discovery. As part of this you could engage with the following enquiries and suggested activities. Use your journal to write down your thoughts, feelings and responses.

CONSIDER THESE QUESTIONS, ASK YOURSELF:

- What big vision do you have for your life?

- In what areas of your life are you failing to convey your vision effectively?

- What does freedom mean to you?

- What do you put your faith in? What does God, or the Divine, mean to you?

- In what ways do you overshoot the mark, get things out of proportion, misjudge the size of things?

SUGGESTED EXERCISES AND ACTIVITIES

- Do the big-picture visioning exercise, the walk and the vision, as described above.

- Think about an important mentor in your life, someone who inspired you to be more than you thought you could be, to achieve more than you thought was possible. Connect with the mentor that now exists as an archetype in your own psyche. Call upon that figure for guidance.

- Consider working with a life coach to support you in your visioning process.

- Visit a cathedral, a mosque, an ashram, a temple, or a place in nature that you find spiritually uplifting. Spend some time there; experience the awe that it inspries in you and allow it to expand your faith in some way.

The Tenth Gateway

Capricorn

Sun in Capricorn period: *21/22 December – 20/21 January*

Symbol: *The Goat-Fish*

Motivation: *Cardinal/initiating*

Element (temperament): *Earth*

Ruling planets: *Saturn*

Body part ruled: *Knees*

Keynote: *I stand. I endure. I succeed.*

Version of the truth: *Is it achievable? Will it stand the test of time?*

Medicine: *Integrity. Accountability. Dedication.*

Shadow energy: *Ruthless ambition. Abuse of power. Ends justify means.*

Mantra: *I carry the wisdom of the elders and the strength to complete the task I am set.*

The transition from Sagittarius to Capricorn

The transition by element from fire to earth involves the incarnation and incorporation of Spirit. It draws the life force into the body, and the reality check it confronts us with in this sign shift is especially apparent. The adventure of Sagittarius has reignited our imagination with the passion to journey beyond the bounds of what we had previously thought possible. Now that we have reached the Winter Solstice in the calendar, the pinnacle of the zodiacal circle, it is Capricorn's job to make us accountable for our high aspirations, help us ground our expanded vision in the world and align us to our purpose. Capricorn medicine reins in the excesses of our questing aspirations and far-flung passions, reminding us of the limitations of our physical being. It also lays down a challenge: *You've come here to do something with your life, so what are you doing about it?* Capricorn insists that you have a destiny, that there is something you were born to do, and it demands you step up, make a stand, and commit to a vocation in life. The wild freedoms of Sagittarius are now harnessed, both by the constraints of the physical body and its lifespan, and within the structured intention of a life's unfolding plan. This, in turn, is conditioned by expectations, both from society and our own soul, that we are supposed to make something of our lives. Sagittarius is the preparatory phase, where we are given the space and freedom to explore possibilities and respond to what inspires our joy and lifts our hearts. Capricorn calls that vision to account and sets about turning it into a mission statement for our lives. Through Sagittarius, Jupiter expanded you, and now Capricorn's ruler, Saturn, contracts you. Its role is to reduce the scope of your wandering eye, focus your exploration, and train your idealism to make it conform to a definite path, then get you to commit to it.

What is your destination?

There is a wide world out there and we could spend our whole lives traversing it, yet it is only a speck in a universe whose vastness we can only visualise because of the immense scope of our imagination. There are infinite possibilities available to us, journeys without end. It must have been a Sagittarian who came up with the phrase, *the journey is more important than the destination.* Yet Capricorn requires us to have an end goal in order to give us orientation and keep us focused on where we are going. Where are you going? What path are you following, and what is the destination that keeps you on track?

In 2012, I walked El Camino de Santiago de Compostela, a 780-kilometre pilgrimage across northern Spain. It was a profoundly life-altering experience for me, and its Sagittarian medicine enabled me to see my life from a completely different perspective and get an expanded view of what my life was for. But as a Capricornian experience, it also taught me a great deal about patience and step-by-step endurance; it inspired in me the commitment to see something through. I underwent a lot of physical pain and discomfort, but the promise of Santiago looming in the distance kept me going and the sense of achievement I felt upon arrival has stayed with me, and it has grounded my aspirations.

Do you sense that you have a mission here on Earth? And if there is a purpose to your life, a destiny that you are meant to fulfil, how committed are you to seeing it through? Carry this in mind as the wheel turns again now, and sense the *gravitas* of that question as we enter the tenth gateway.

The cardinal earth sign

Capricorn completes the earthy triad in the zodiac wheel. In Taurus the earth element gave us food, resources and natural abilities. In Virgo we got to work with the earth and the body; we became apprenticed, developed skills to harvest that potential and practices to keep us connected within the weave of life. In Capricorn, we must now acknowledge our experience and readiness to structure that developed capacity of the earth element and establish it as a 'concrete assignment that demands fulfilment'.[1] Capricorn also completes the zodiacal cycle of cardinal signs, marking the fourth of the major turning points in the calendar. Cardinal energy initiates and gives directional impetus to the element that animates it. First Aries gave us a baptism of fire, then watery Cancer provoked an emotional response drawn from the wellspring of memory, next Libra initiated us culturally and directed us towards social engagements. Now that cardinal initiative becomes fully embodied in matter, calling for a substantial step to be taken towards some definite outcome. Capricorn harnesses us to a sense of duty and responsibility, prompting us to gather all the experience of our soul's journey, not just in this life, but over aeons of time, directing that with purpose and intent.

The goat-fish

Like Sagittarius, the constellation of Capricorn offers another composite figure: a goat-fish, a creature with a goat's head and front legs, and a fish's tail. The image has its origins in Mesopotamia as the God Ea (Greek Oannes), who had a human form cloaked in a fish's skin. This great being of wisdom, vision and vast intellect is said to have risen from the sea, bringing forth the gift of civilisation to humanity. Also called the father of light, he periodically reincarnates during periods of crisis or cultural/spiritual transition in order to instruct humankind.[2] He was also known as the 'antelope of the subterranean ocean'[3] and was said to have adopted the form of a goat whenever he roamed the Earth. The goat, and sometimes antelope, is depicted nibbling on the leaves of the great Tree of Life.[4]

The authority of the 'Unconquerable Sun'

Capricorn marks the Winter Solstice, and the return of the light. In the wheel it opposes Cancer, which nurtured our humanity and marked the Summer Solstice, the gateway of matter and of ordinary human incarnation. Capricorn now marks the so-called gateway of spirit, through which the masters, the initiated teachers of humanity, were said to take physical form.[5] In state-sponsored Roman paganism dating to the third century CE, *Dies Natalis Solis Invicti* – 'the birthday of the Unconquerable Sun' – was celebrated each year on 25 December.[6] This is the first day when the rising Sun visibly begins to shift northwards along the eastern horizon, indicating the first increase in the length of day after three days of solar standstill. The celebration of Christ's birth on this day is surely a deliberate reference to this cult and, although concrete evidence is lacking, it does suggest a possible lineage of solstice-born avatar figures whose mythic role is to lead humanity out of darkness into the light.[7] It is also conceivable that Roman emperors customarily granted themselves a second birthday on 25 December, based on the fact that they had themselves represented as a goat-fish, thus identifying themselves with the sign of Capricorn and associating themselves the authority of the *Sol Invictus*.[8]

The scapegoat

People born under the sign of Capricorn are renowned for their capacity and apparent willingness to take on more than their fair share of responsibility, and can find themselves being scapegoated in one way or another when things go wrong. We think of a scapegoat as someone singled out for unreasonably harsh treatment on behalf of some wider societal or organisational failing, the one who *takes the rap*. This idea originates with the Jewish tradition of *azazel*, whereby a goat was cast into the desert as part of the ceremonies on the Day of Atonement. Each year on a certain day, two goats would be presented at the door of the tabernacle, as a way of dealing with the corporeal sins of God's chosen people. One, the 'Lord's Goat', would be sacrificed, its blood sprinkled on the so-called 'mercy seat' behind the veil in the Holy of Holies; the other, the *azazel* or scapegoat, would be driven into the wilderness, taking the sins of the people with it.[9] The Jewish Day of Atonement foreshadows the role of Christ, who is sometimes referred to in theology as the scapegoat, and who Christians believe died for the sins of humanity. His crucifixion removes the need for the annual animal sacrifice, as he is thought to have fulfilled the role himself, once and for all. Again we see the Capricorn symbolism at play.

The sensuous power of the goat

The constellation of Capricorn was seen by the Greeks as the horned, goat-footed god, Pan, the lusty, nature-loving deity who roams the meadows and hillsides of Arcadia playing his enchanting pipes. To escape the wrath of Typhon, Pan leaped into the River Nile. As he did so his head was transformed into that of a goat, remaining above water, while his lower, immersed half became a fish-tail.[10] So we find a profound paradox at the heart of this sign's symbolism. With all its aptitude for spiritual enlightenment, Capricorn is a deeply sensuous earth sign and the attraction of the spiritual being towards the material experience is never more intense than here. The early Church fathers turned the pagan Pan into their cloven-hoofed devil, although his image has since been reclaimed by romantic poets, writers and philosophers who praised this ancient god of shepherds, flocks and mountain wilds, of rustic wisdom and enchanting music. For Shelley, Pan comes as 'the wind in the reeds and the rushes';[11] he is Keats's 'forester divine';[12] Kenneth Grahame's 'piper at the gates of dawn';[13] for William Blake, 'the lust of the goat is the bounty of God'.[14] It is a goat-nymph, Amalthea, who rears the infant Zeus, her milk giving him the strength to become the greatest of the gods. Zeus creates his thunder-shield, or *aegis*, from Amalthea's goat-hide and fashions the 'horn of plenty', or *cornucopia*, from her crown.[15] Goat medicine, it is said, bestows long-lived endurance, abundance and sexual potency.

Heaven and Earth united

In the Christian era, all these pagan images that venerate the carnal aspect of creation have been treated with fear, guilt and suspicion. Freed from such prejudice, however, Capricorn can be seen as Spirit penetrating deep into the erotic heart of Nature, in search of the abiding, passionate union of Heaven and Earth, one that reveals both the goddess and the god and celebrates the consummation of their love. In this ultimate communion of Father Sky and Mother Earth, abstract Spirit finds a home in sensuous matter, with the incorporated power of Nature aspiring to meet it. The strikingly pagan ritual of bringing a spruce tree into our homes at Christmas captures this idea perfectly. It remembers the evergreen Yggdrasil, the world tree that maintains cosmic order, the *axis mundi* that links the upper, middle and lower worlds. It reaches beyond Asgard, the home of the gods, to hold up the sky and all stars.[16] The world was seen as hanging by a mighty thread from the great, immortal stars of the celestial North Pole, which never rose or set, and around which the whole cosmos turned. It was also seen as a great mill churning out gold and all the wealth of creation, the source of all life and order.[17] The Greeks knew this to be the *Omphalloessa* and located its earthly counterpart at Delphi; the Romans called it the *Umbilicus* and located it in Rome. In the body it is where the umbilical cord stems from, the point we call the navel. The Babylonians knew it as the 'mother bond of heaven' and it is our route back to the mother, where we humans instinctively imagine our centre to be.[18] It is a point of centredness, from which a shaft of energy connects the above and the below via an axial pillar of light or world tree.

Time and integrity

As befits the midwinter season, Capricorn is a hardy, practical sign. It can be dour and determinedly grim, the cold weather tending to dry the skin, contract the muscles and harden the bones. The figures from myth that emerge are Father Winter or Old Father Time, who remind us of the inevitable demise of the physical form. This is one of the names of Saturn (Greek Cronos), planetary

ruler of Capricorn, who checks our stride and keeps us in time and in order, commanding respect and discipline, insisting that we employ a long-term strategy and stick to it. Saturn demands his pound of flesh and often materialises in our lives as an authority figure who scrutinises our efforts and puts us to the test to see how serious we are in our ambitions.

Two-headed Janus, a god of doorways and transitions, presides over the New Year, looking forward and back, acting as the hinge connecting what is past with what is to come.[19] In the same way, Capricorn sees far enough ahead and behind to formulate a long-term directive. With the emphasis on slow and steady progress, it provides the foresight to endure and the hindsight to know that things take the time that they take to manifest. This medicine demands that you examine your relationship with time, and the bearing that has on your integrity and the power of your word. Here's a practice which sounds absurdly simple but for many of us involves a profound shift of orientation: make some definite commitments, establish some actions you need to take that are realistically achievable, and set a time when you will do them. Then simply do them, at the time that you said you would. Get others involved and ask them to support you, to hold you to account in some way. Keep doing this and notice what happens.

Authority and the law

With Saturn at the helm, the hardy goat takes charge of the mission, bears responsibility for what happens along the way and ensures that every action is met with an appropriate consequence. Saturn holds us accountable for our thoughts and actions as a way of bringing balance to the soul.[20] He is the record-keeper who upholds the law, in society, in nature and the cosmos. So this is an appropriate moment in the journey to consider your own relationship to the law. To who or what do you look for authority? Whose law(s) do you respect and give credence to? To what extent do you trust the integrity of those who assume power in the world? How do you position yourself within the political structures of your society? What spiritual authority do you acknowledge or revere? Do you perhaps look more to nature and natural laws for guidance as to how to act appropriately in the world? These are important questions to ask as we move into the final quadrant of the wheel. We are asked to step up now, in some way, as an authority in our own right, and this increases our power in the world as well as our ability to influence things. Many people shy away from this because of their issues with power; but to authentically express this medicine, we need to address this question as to what power and authority means to us.

The Capricorn shadow: 'The end justifies the means'

Capricorn is a medicine of power, and it carries a powerful shadow. One only need look at the hierarchical structure of our religious, political and economic institutions, all thoroughly Capricornian in nature. Whether or not they were originally designed to serve the healthy functioning of our communities and society as a whole, most of them have, at some point, been corrupted by a lust for power and control that infiltrates the heart of their administrative set-up, from the leaders who wield the power to the adherents who submit to it. In most cases, those in government, big business and positions of religious authority create and enforce laws that will maintain and reinforce the structures that support their own interests, usually at the expense of those they are mandated to serve. This Capricornian shadow points to a weakness that almost every human being carries at some level in their relationship to power. We want to feel empowered, but we don't want others to have power over us. There is something extremely attractive about power, but at the same time it can be deeply repulsive to us, and when a person's ego structure is weak, they cannot handle it one way or the other.

Power struggles characterise so many relationships, families and communities. We like to think that we know what is best for another person, for the family, for society and we will objectify those views and take up a position of authority. The Capricorn shadow will rally our opinions, fixate our judgements and make us intolerant of others' views, so convinced are we that we know best. We act as if it's our duty to make others change, demand obedience within the family or pursue power as a way of influencing society. In the process we become blind to our own behaviours, so focused on the end result that we disregard the means we employ to get there. The same thing can happen with personal ambition. We might ruthlessly pursue a career goal and do anything to meet that target, driven by that mantra, *the end justifies the means.*

Too much or too little Capricorn

If you are overburdened with Capricorn medicine or have a particularly strong Saturnian nature, you may need to really have a look at your relationship to power and authority, your motives for doing things, what success means to you and what you would and wouldn't be prepared to do in order to achieve your goals. Another manifestation would be to take life too seriously, forget to play, work too hard or take more than your fair share of responsibility on your shoulders. You may find that others look to you because they know you are strong and you can handle it. You may be prone to periods of melancholy, and/or disappointment when life doesn't live up to your expectations. You are also realistic, though, and part of your practice is to learn tolerance, both for yourself and for others. The practice of humility is good medicine for a strong Capricorn type. Capricorn rules the knees, and when the true initiate has climbed the mountain, achieved some form of enlightenment or realised her destiny, she kneels. If you lack access to Capricorn energy, you might find yourself more reluctant to step up into positions of responsibility, be shy of power or lack the persistence and dedication to see things through to the end. You may find yourself frustrated that your plans don't come to fruition or that you don't reach your goal. Take a healthy dose of this medicine if you recognise this in yourself. Focus on aligning yourself to some longer-term goals, clarifying the steps you need to take to achieve them, then taking a definite first step.

North Star alignment

During the Capricorn workshop on *The Alchemical Journey* we invite participants to connect with the Heaven-Earth axis by making an alignment to the North Star. Close your eyes and imagine a pillar of light linking the centre within your body to the pole star at the centre of the heavens, simultaneously extending downwards to the core of the Earth. Hold this alignment, focus on the North Star and imagine the other stars and constellations turning slowly around you. Feel this continual parade while remaining anchored in the experience of centredness, a dynamic stillness that exists in the core of the heavens, in the core of the Earth, in the core of your being. Stay with this for a few minutes; then, coming out of that meditation, draw a picture of your North Star in your journal. Consider what it means for you in terms of your purpose and direction in life, and write down anything that comes to you. Having done that, draw a square on another page with four pillars, one at each corner. Imagine this is your personal temple for grounding your North Star vision, an earthly container capable of housing, supporting and bounding your North Star aspiration. Imagine that each pillar represents a core value or principle that helps to align and ground you, practically and ethically, in the world. Write down a core value at each corner of the square, feel into the moral integrity of that and the strength that it gives you. Spend some time visualising yourself embodying these four principles and inhabiting this temple of your being, always aligned to the star that holds the key to your purpose and destiny.

Capricorn summary

Spend time during this tenth stage of the wheel looking at your life as a whole and what you want to do with it. Could there be purpose to your existence? Do you have a destiny and, if so, what are you doing about it? Engage with the following enquiries and suggested activities. Use your journal, write down your thoughts, feelings and responses, and be prepared to really examine yourself through this medicine.

CONSIDER THESE QUESTIONS,
ASK YOURSELF:

- What does success mean to you, and how do you measure it?

- What is your stand in the world? What do you stand for?

- What stops you stepping up or making a stand?

- What is your relationship to authority? Who or what do you give authority to?

- In what areas of life do you lack direction or purpose?

- Where do you need to establish better boundaries in your life?

- When you commit to something, do you deliver?

SUGGESTED ACTIVITIES

- Do the 'North Star alignment' exercise discussed above.

- Practise the 'Time and Integrity' exercise: doing what you said, when you said you would.

- Make a list of your accomplishments – things you've achieved in your life – acknowledge yourself and notice any responses from within. Then make another list of the things you will still want to accomplish in your life.

- Make a list of the things that you believe limit you in life, conditions that you imagine shape and structure what is possible for you. Examine your relationship to these and clarify which are actually true (some will be) and which are just excuses for not stepping up!

The Eleventh Gateway

Aquarius

Sun in Aquarius period: *20/21 January – 20/21 February*

Symbol: *The Water Bearer*

Motivation: *Fixed/establishing and maintaining*

Element (temperament): *Air*

Ruling planets: *Saturn and Uranus*

Body parts ruled: *Calves and ankles, blood circulation*

Keynote: *I innovate, design and sustain the systems of life.*

Version of the truth: *Will it serve humanity's future?*

Medicine: *Higher perspectives. Inclusion. Rejuvenation.*

Shadow energy: *Coldness. Heartless systems.*

Mantra: *I enable the waters of life to flow, in service to humanity's highest vision.*

The transition from Capricorn to Aquarius

If you have done your Capricorn labour, you will have restored your integrity, clarified your stand and realised your mission in life. You may feel as if you have arrived, but the wheel is a great teacher now. Capricorn may be the highest sign, the sign of achievement, but it is quite evidently not the end of the zodiacal journey. We have two signs left, both signs of service, and both are more interested in the ways in which we are connected than in your personal successes! Having knelt humbly at the peak of self-realisation, it is now time to head back down the mountain and serve humanity. As you enter Aquarius, you have a wide view of the world spread out below you. From this vantage point, you might be able to see how things interrelate, to glimpse something of the greater plan, get a proper overview of things. Take this time to see into your own future, for while your personal ambition might be sated, your opportunity to make a genuine contribution in the world may just be unfolding before you. You have distinguished yourself in Capricorn, but in order to make the difference, this superior understanding must reach with humility into the ordinary moments of life, where communities gather around everyday needs. You have the opportunity to give back now, and as your own cup is filled, so let its contents spill over and nourish others. You are the water-bearer now, and you can be a river to your people.[1]

Making a difference

There is a distinct shift of vibration as we enter Aquarius. This wheel is turning elementally from earth to air and we must lighten the load that we carry. This is also the moment when we realise the potential of the whole rainbow spectrum of colour within us, and we become emissaries of light. In order to do this, we must release the burden of responsibility that we have borne in Capricorn. In the film *The Mission*, the mercenary and slaver, Rodrigo Mendoza (played by Robert de Niro), climbs a sheer mountain in the Paraguayan jungle dragging a heavy bundle of armour behind him as a self-chosen penance to atone for the guilt associated with his past actions. He endures until he reaches a high plateau when he falls to his knees in tearful humility before the tribe of natives who have suffered at his hands and to whom he will end up dedicating himself in service. They cut him loose of his burden. What burden of duty or guilt are you carrying on your shoulders that might be preventing you from serving the world in the way that you could? Think about the contribution that you make or want to make to your community, to society, to the planet. In what way could you shift your focus from the more isolated perspective of being obligated, and towards the more inclusive recognition of your shared humanity? Consider your inter-dependence within the community you choose to serve and, as you enter the Aquarian gateway, ask yourself: *What makes me different and what difference do I make?*

The Water Carrier

The symbol for this sign shows two wavy lines, the traditional symbol for water; however, this is not a water sign. Like a river, Aquarius is the vessel that carries the water, it is not the water itself. This sign's commitment to the life-sustaining network and its non-attachment to the emotional content renders Aquarius uniquely capable of bearing the chalice for humanity. What is borne in that sacred cup and the way it is received will depend on the level of consciousness of the society that it is designed to serve. Aquarius completes the airy triad of signs. The Geminian impulse for language and social exchange matured in Libra through the attraction of opposites and the dance of partnership. Now the air element seeks form throughout the wider community, as ideas become established as ideals. As the final fixed sign of the zodiac, Aquarius can establish, stabilise and maintain structures through creating ethical and innovative social and organisational templates for society. Traditionally ruled by Saturn, it gives form to ideas that can encourage debate and inclusion of different viewpoints, tending more towards democratic and egalitarian ideals than hierarchical governance.

First stirrings of the light

The Sun enters Aquarius in the tropical zodiac around 20 January. It is winter in the northern hemisphere, and in many places water has frozen to ice. In the outer manifest world

there is little apparent life, except for the
enthusiastic communities of snowdrops
that grace our gardens. At the same time,
we begin to sense the accelerated increase
of daylight in early February.[2] To me the
snowdrop is the perfect Aquarian flower:
white, pure, ahead of its time, a torch
bearer. The beginning of February is also
the time when the light-bringer Brigid is

remembered, her candle flame kept alight at her cult centre in
Kildare; an old Irish legend even claims her to have been a
wet-nurse of the infant Christ. Christianity marks this as the
'Feast of Lights' or Candlemas, when the Virgin Mary first
presents Jesus at the Temple in Jerusalem, offering herself to be
purified forty days after giving birth. This corresponds, in the
pagan calendar, with the festival of *Imbolc*, meaning 'sheep's
milk'.[3] At this time of year ewes begin to lactate, prior to the
lambing season (when the Sun is in Aries). There is a readying
for new life, felt throughout the natural world and within the
soul. These first stirrings bring forth a sense of hope, a quick-
ening of ideas, a formulation of plans, an ideal design for the
future.

The life-giving waters of Aquarius

The constellation of Aquarius shows a figure pouring water
from a jug. For the Egyptians, this was Hapi, a male god
usually depicted with a pendulous belly and a woman's

breasts.[4] Vegetation grows out of his head and he holds two vases, each pouring forth water. Hapi was god of the Nile, Egypt's immense, sacred river that would burst its banks annually in July and August, when the full moon rises in Aquarius at sunset. As the Nile flooded the land on either side, bringing up rich silt from its bed, it would create two bands of fertile soil in an otherwise barren desert. This inundation was a blessing from the goddess Isis, embodied in the star we know today as Sirius; it would return to the night sky each year at this time, with Aquarius being the last constellation to set before sunrise.[5] The Egyptians would have seen Hapi dipping his urn into the great river, displacing the water and causing it to burst forth onto the land, a sign of abundance and good fortune.[6] When we thank our lucky stars we honour Aquarius, a constellation which contains the two luckiest stars in the sky, remembered by their Arab names, Sadalmelek and Sadalsuud.[7]

Delilah the water bearer

The Leonine solar hero, Samson, finds his Aquarian counterpart in Delilah, whose name means 'water pitcher' or 'she of Aquarius'.[8] Like Hercules, Samson draws his strength from the long rays of the summer Sun, represented in his strong head of hair, the great pride of Leo. Delilah diminishes his strength by cutting his hair, and is viewed in the biblical account as his betrayer; yet the act equally reflects her Aquarian role in the seasonal mystery, as the hair-cutting reflects the shortened, weaker rays of the wintertime Sun.[9] The Sun is said to be in detriment in this sign, yet it is Delilah who carries the flowing waters that represent the renewal of life. In a famous grisaille panel, Samson and Delilah are shown lying beneath a dead tree with a luxuriant vine wrapped around it – suggesting the fruitfulness of a woman in her prime – and a fountain that overflows and seeps away into the ground.[10] These paired opposites bestow fundamental gifts of life: Leo as the vital Sun, Aquarius as the rain-bearing clouds. Leo rules the heart while Aquarius governs the circulatory system, ensuring a flow of return to the heart, which stimulates the brain and keeps the mind lively and active. Where Leo is heart-centred, Aquarius is mind-centred and promotes the healthy maintenance of the network, its energy channelled into maintaining the flow between all constituent members of a system, community or society.

The fountain of youth

The Greek gods, high on Mount Olympus, originally employed a young woman, Hebe, daughter of Zeus and Hera, as their Aquarian cupbearer. Her Roman name, Juventas, means 'eternally youthful', and she delivered the divine *ambrosia*, the elixir of immortality. The story goes that she slipped one day, spilling the ambrosia and exposing her nakedness; this was said to have embarrassed the gods, so she was replaced by Ganymede, a beautiful young Trojan boy whom Zeus abducted while in the guise of an eagle. It is Ganymede who is placed in the heavens as the Aquarius constellation we know today.[11]

Hebe's dismissal for sexual exposure strikes us as odd, but it is almost certainly a patriarchal alteration, indicating a shift away from emphasis on the life-sustaining abundance of the goddess. Older stories from Egypt and Sumeria tell of the healing powers associated with the exposure of the sacred genitalia of the goddesses Hathor and Ninhursag, which may hint at the origin of Hebe's role.[12] Interestingly, Hebe becomes Hercules's wife after the hero wins his immortality. As with Delilah and Samson, the strength and solar power of Leo finds its balancing force in a female deity who is the rejuvenating fountain of youth and bestower of the elixir of everlasting life.

The creativity within living systems

According to scientist Fritjof Capra, living systems in nature continuously 'renew and recycle their components while maintaining the integrity of their overall structure', while also having the ability to transcend themselves, 'to reach out creatively beyond physical and mental boundaries in the processes of learning, development and evolution'.[13] Living systems theory acknowledges a certain determinism of shaping by environmental factors, but includes the agency of free will and innovation as the level of autonomy within a living system increases. This finds its expression in the complexity of human culture. As human awareness increases, so, apparently, does our capacity to innovate. This captures the spirit of Aquarius perfectly. Being a sign of organisational coherence, in line with the more deterministic dictates of its ruler, Saturn, it is equally a sign of originality, eccentricity and independence, befitting its modern ruler, Uranus.

The spirit of revolution

William Herschel's discovery of Uranus in 1781 had a huge impact on the collective psyche. The discovery of a new planet beyond the bounds of Saturn revolutionised astronomy and disrupted the elegant order that had existed in the heavens for millennia. It was a testament to the rise of science and the supposed genius of the Enlightenment, reflecting a new spirit of human innovation. It coincided with political and industrial revolutions, breakthroughs in philosophical understanding, and radical cultural developments that appeared to liberate mankind from the harsh injunctions of natural law. It seemed to expose religious faith as superstition and the authority of the Church was undermined as a new, iconoclastic humanism emerged. The French and American revolutions turned existing systems of government on their heads in the hope of establishing a more egalitarian society. We can see why Uranus would eventually be given rulership over Aquarius;[14] that idealistic part in each of us seeks a radical solution to the inequity of Saturnian hierarchy and control. Through this medicine we seek to discern the unchanging platonic forms of life that lie behind the flux of phenomena that manifest in the world.[15] Aquarius holds the keys to that invisible network of information that dynamically creates life, society and culture.

Uranus and Prometheus

In myth, Uranus (Greek Ouranos) was the sky god, firstborn of Gaia, the Earth Mother. He poured down rains upon her so that she would become verdant and flourish, then mated with her to produce the race of Titans, the gods and goddesses who came to rule over humankind. Richard Tarnas points out that while this mythological theme fits certain aspects of the astrological Uranus (and by extension Aquarius), the Titan god Prometheus is a more authentic carrier of Uranian energy.[16] Prometheus is said to have fashioned the first humans from clay, becoming their great champion and rebelling against Zeus who had withheld from them the gift of fire. Climbing to the top of Mount Olympus, he was able to catch a spark of divine fire on a fennel stalk, as Helios flashed past in his chariot. He gave this to humanity, granting them the power of imagination, innovation and foresight. It was judged by the other gods to be the ultimate *hubris* and he was severely punished.[17] Being ahead of their time, Aquarians often suffer for their misunderstood ideas and sometimes fail to gain recognition for their genius in their own lifetimes.

Pandora's Box

As a consequence of the theft of fire, an angry Zeus instructed the smith-god Hephaestus to create Pandora, together with her famous box (or jar), and sent her as a gift to Prometheus's brother, Epimetheus. Pandora carries certain Aquarian paradoxes; being of human form, but forged from Olympian fire and adorned with all the charms of a goddess; possessed of divine beauty, but also, we are told, a vacuous and absent-minded nature. She is instructed never to open the box, but curiosity gets the better of her. Despite far-seeing Prometheus's best efforts to warn his brother, all the ills of the world are let loose upon humanity through her negligence: old age, labour, sickness, insanity, vice and passion. One thing remains, though, hope: the hope of redemption, salvation, that things will improve, that darkness, fear and ignorance can be overcome, healed or transcended. Pandora, when fully realised as the Aquarian goddess of healing that she is, holds the key to this restoration.

Pandora and the Star

The Tarot card of the Star, trump XVI, is attributed to Aquarius.[18] The Rider-Waite image depicts a female figure pouring water from a vase into a pool of water.[19] In Crowley's Thoth deck, the woman is far more sensuously immersed in the act of libation, like an ecstatic dancer being restored at the fountain of youth.[20] In Greene and Sharman-Burke's Mythic Tarot, this trump depicts Pandora in her Aquarian form, with the star of hope.[21] Pandora is a more complex figure than her story suggests. Her name means the 'all-giver', or 'all-gifted', and she is the diviner of earthly wisdom, complete within herself. Robert Graves tells us that Pandora's jar originally contained winged souls, which were liberated upon its opening.[22] He argues that the true contents of her sacred

casket belong to the mysteries of the divine feminine, and
carry power and benevolence if their secrets are respected.
Graves points to a inversion of the same myth, featuring
Demophon (consort of Pandora's acolyte, Phyllis) whose
curiosity causes *him* to open the casket and he is driven mad
by what he finds there; 'a warning to men who pry into
women's mysteries'[23] with their wandering curiosity and
restless penchant for invention.

The Aquarian shadow: disembodiment

The warnings inherent in the Pandora story point us towards
the Aquarian shadow energy. We all have a side of us that
thinks we can design a better world. We all want to make
things better for our communities and this is a fine and
admirable aspiration. However, if we are ever to thrive as a
culture, we must hold open a compassionate space in our
imaginations for the messy, spilled-out contents of Pandora's
vessel. Any system that divorces itself from the natural cycles
of return, any organisation that tries to declare itself immune
to sickness, vice, decay and death, cuts itself off from the
waters of rejuvenation that are so vital to its sustainability.
Only a society that respects and nourishes all of its members
can function sustainably, and likewise for the healthy integration of the psyche with its pantheon of archetypes. Inclusion
and the acceptance of difference are among Aquarius's most
merit-worthy attributes, but this is often approached from a
safe theoretical distance. Delilah's waters must flow back into

the earth if we are to be truly nourished back to health, with community grown up from its grass roots. Pandora is a chthonic goddess; her deep earth wisdom is at odds with the hierarchical order of Olympus, to whom she becomes enslaved at a time of treachery and mistrust among the patriarchal gods who have designs upon humanity. This is the tension and challenge we inevitably face in Aquarius, when we get swept up in marvellous plans which look good on paper but are sometimes too rigid and unwieldy in practice.

The heartless system

The essence of the Aquarian shadow is the heartless system, with everything assembled according to elegantly designed principles, and set up in a way that it is unresponsive to the inconsistencies, inefficiencies and unpredictabilities that characterise the way people actually live. We hold out great hope for the coming astrological Age of Aquarius, that it will bring a more enlightened perspective, promoting peace, unity and brother/sisterhood. But perhaps it is already here, masquerading as an abstract, disenchanted consumerism fuelled by technological innovation, with the internet now acting as a disembodied double of Pandora's mythic vessel.[24] It provides the theoretical framework of community, yet it can leave us feeling empty inside if it does not connect with the restorative power of sensuously lived experience.

Too much or too little Aquarius

We love Aquarians because they give us the space to be ourselves and tend not to take things too personally, often considering the good of the group over the needs of the individual. An over-reliance on this, however, can make you appear distant and aloof, either tending towards anonymity or else becoming so eccentric that people find it hard to get close to you. You may place a high value on objectivity, grand meta-narratives, top-down 'design view' ways of approaching problems. Your ideas may be endlessly fascinating, but how effectively do you apply them in the world and contribute to society in the way you would like? Are your thoughts and words connecting with where people are really at? Are they touching people's hearts? If you lack much access to the Aquarian perspective, you may find it more difficult to get that wider overview of things, struggle to find that space within yourself to see things clearly. If you find yourself too central to situations, too easily embroiled in emotional dramas, bogged down with the tedium of mundane affairs in situations which demand your attention, take time to inhale the rich aromas of this medicine. Create more space in your life; focus more on your ideals; expand your view of the future; contemplate the difference that you could make to it.

Aquarian medicine: the round-table perspective

Aquarian medicine gives us the ability to glimpse the web of life, the interconnected matrix of relationships that set the template for manifest existence; the sacred geometry of life, the ideal formulations of number, shape and pattern. If we can engage with this energy and release its power in our lives, it can put us in touch with our highest human potential, our capacity to work creatively for the good of the whole. Aquarius offers us a unique glimpse of the crystalline structure of creation, reflected beautifully in the geometry of the zodiac itself. With its twelve multi-faceted perspectives perfectly interwoven in the round wheel, it creates a whole infinitely more powerful than the sum of its parts. Each sign has its place and its unique contribution to make; each can learn from the other, recognising and honouring different strengths and areas of expertise, fostering qualities of interdependence and cooperation. This is the round-table ideal. As part of the Aquarius workshop on *The Alchemical Journey* we set up a council of twelve and we imagine a scenario where we gather as a group to address a pressing social or environmental issue. Each person embodies one of the zodiac perspectives; with a talking stick, each member has their opportunity to step forward, express their truth and be heard. Aquarius encapsulates the principle of unity-in-diversity, the realisation that together we shine as one light but our true beauty, like a rainbow, manifests only when its complete spectrum of colour is revealed.

Aquarius summary

Spend time during this eleventh stage of the wheel contemplating the ideological template of your life and your vision of a better world. Work with the following enquiries and suggested activities. Write your thoughts, feelings and responses in your journal, and prepare to really examine yourself through this medicine.

CONSIDER THESE QUESTIONS, ASK YOURSELF:

- What makes you stand out from the crowd? What's your genius?

- What difference do you make, or could you make, in the world?

- Are you giving yourself enough abstract thinking space (or too much, or too little)?

- In what ways might you be keeping yourself distant and aloof, or avoiding real human contact?

- Locate your personal 'fountain of youth'. What rejuvenates you and restores your vitality?

SUGGESTED EXERCISES AND ACTIVITIES

- Make a list, or, better, a mind map of the groups (social or political), clubs, boards, associations and communities that you belong to or are involved with. See how they connect together and identify the roles that you play in them.

- If there is a group, team or family set-up in which you play an indispensable central role, practise stepping back yourself in some way that enables everyone in that group to have a more equal voice.

- If there is a project that you want to move forward, reach out to others in your community to come together and share your vision with them, seek out collaboration, invite other perspectives.

The Twelfth Gateway

Pisces

Sun in Pisces period: *20/21 February – 20/21 March*

Symbol: *The Fishes*

Motivation: *Mutable/adapting and transforming*

Element (temperament): *Water*

Ruling planets: *Jupiter, Neptune*

Body part ruled: *Feet*

Keynote: *I feel it all. I give up. I unite. We are one.*

Version of the truth: *Does it include everything? Does it touch the deepest part of the soul?*

Medicine: *Compassion. Poetry. Unconditional love.*

Shadow energy: *Addiction. Escapism. Confusion. Deception.*

Mantra: *I am not separate. I am one with all beings.*

The transition from Aquarius to Pisces

The world may appear unusually clear right now. We have pierced the veil of manifest reality and glimpsed the archetypal structure of creation lying behind it. We have peeked inside the mind of the Great Architect, awestruck by the geometric elegance of the 'Grand Design'. Yet as we transition from the spatial awareness of Aquarius to the immersive waters of Pisces, this matrix, this formal abstraction of consciousness, is set to dissolve back into the dream from whence it emerged. The highly taut threads of reason that seemed so perfectly delineated are loosened now. Certainties will merge back into their original condition of entanglement, the very idea of objective reality undermined. Our capacity to discern subject from object, perceiver from perceived, becomes more of a mystery as concepts unravel to reveal their inevitable perceptual bias. The definition in our thinking blurs as our minds are inundated with a rich stream of images from the soul. Piscean Albert Einstein recognised that knowledge is limited, while 'imagination encircles the world'.[1] Sometimes the studied articulation of our prose fails us and we are lost to the baffling ambiguities of existence; only then does life become the poem that it was always meant to be.

Letting go

Aquarius has revealed to us the interconnectedness of all things and the interrelatedness of all beings. It has presented us with a map, through which we can perceive the conceptual structure of the wheel as an enlightened model for both psyche and society. Yet it does not complete the wheel of our being. For that we must return to the realm of water, to the soulful and irreconcilable yearning that no map can ever comprehend or hope to encompass. What is it that you long for beyond all else? After all that you have been through, in all the lifetimes you may have known, what calls your soul home? Can you even express it in words? At an Aquarian level, this life you are living now is an elegantly constructed choreography, mapped out in the star patterns of your birth. As a dancer you have had to learn the steps, but there comes a moment when you simply let go and surrender your mind to the deeper current of feeling that flows through you. Then there is only the dance. Notice the extent to which you cling to ideas, concepts and ideological structures and, as you enter the twelfth and final gateway of Pisces, ask yourself: *What if I just let go ...?*

The sign of the fishes

The Pisces constellation remembers the deities of love, Aphrodite and Eros, who dived into the Euphrates River and turned themselves into fish to escape the warring Titans. A silver cord tied their tails together so they would never lose each other. The cords are bound by the enigmatic star we know as *Al Rischa*, the knot of heaven, *nodus celestis*, a star that has been linked with Christ and the Star of Bethlehem.[2] Christ is represented as a fish in the ancient catacombs of St Callixtus in Rome, and the famous accompanying acronym *ikhthus*, meaning fish, transcribes as 'Jesus-Christ-God-Son-Saviour'.[3] His first followers were fishermen and he famously told Peter 'I will make you fishers of men', prompting artistic depictions of men caught in nets like fish by Christ and his apostles.[4] Even today the Pope still wears the fish-shaped mitre and the New Testament preaches the values that we associate with Pisces: faith, mercy, charity, forgiveness, self-sacrifice and martyrdom.

Waters flowing

Around 20 February each year the Sun enters Pisces in the tropical zodiac, taking us up to the Spring Equinox, as Mother Nature defrosts and softens her brittle wintery edges. As the earth begins to warm, groundwater rises up and rivers flow. Pisces completes the triad of water signs and the cross of mutability. Feelings, memories and impressions drawn from the wellspring in cardinal Cancer, intensified and driven underground in fixed Scorpio, now seep out in all the directions that water may flow wherever the paths of least resistance allow. Raindrops fallen from clouds gather to become 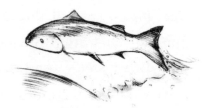 rivulet, stream, river, flowing into the great sea from where the moist air will carry that water back to the clouds. This flow cycle perfectly describes the mutable Piscean nature: always in flux, changing form, shape and direction in an endless search for the sublime.

The longing to transcend

The days are lengthening at an appreciable rate during this phase of the year, and in anticipation of the greening to come, there is a swelling of faith. In agricultural societies winter stocks of food would be almost used up, making this an apt time for fasting. This is Lent in the Christian calendar, the word derived from the Latin *lenten*, which suggests the lengthening of daylight. 'I'm giving it up for Lent', we say. In honour of Christ's forty days in the wilderness, Lent imagines a period of retreat and self-denial in the hope of transcendence or a union with God. Such traditions glisten in the silvery scales of the fishes as we turn away from the everyday concerns of the material world and towards the inner realms of our being. Here we feel the deepest suffering of the soul, the pain of separation, the tearing duality of spirit and matter; yet we also sense our proximity to the ultimate release of suffering and the possibility of spiritual bliss. The two fishes of this constellation are forever connected, but they tug against each other's longing, pulling in different directions. One is bound to the ecliptic and the cyclical ordeal of earthly incarnation, while the other leaps with full faith towards the immortal stars of the north.

Giving it up to the soul

Our twelfth and final zodiacal medicine stirs us to contemplate endings through loss, renunciation and the surrender of personal identity. Pisces is about releasing attachment to the stuff of our everyday lives, giving it up to the soul. We practise this every night when we fall asleep, lose touch with our daytime persona and enter the strange world of dreams. In Virgo we developed practices to sustain and nourish the physical body. In Pisces we nurture and cultivate the soul, our nightly entry into an encounter with Thanatos and, as such, a preparation for death. The soul is distinguished by its special relationship with both the dream and death. It is, as Hillman says, 'the imaginative possibility in our natures',[5] that which lives in us and through us, before us and after us, extended above, below and beyond the limits of our body-bound personality. That temporal container will wither and die like every other living and dying thing. According to most religious teachings in the world, this leaves the soul free to voyage further on its way in search of another vehicle capable of embodying the next episode in its saga of longing.

The oceanic realm of Neptune

That feeling of extension and expansion that we feel in Pisces is synonymous with Jupiter (Greek Zeus), traditional ruling planet of this sign. It is the search for God, the swelling of the mother's belly, the growing anticipation of resurrected life, the gathering waters of Mother Nature in early springtime. Jupiter needs an ally here, though. As a god of height and breadth, he is more naturally responsive to the fiery, upward quest of Sagittarius than the great sea voyage into which Pisces initiates us. For this, Zeus's brother Poseidon (Roman Neptune) is a better fit. The planet Neptune was discovered in the mid-nineteenth century, coinciding with the so-called Romantic era in art, music and literature. This movement was partly a counter-cultural response to the Uranus-themed industrial revolution and enlightenment era of the eighteenth century.[6]

At this time Eastern philosophies, yoga and meditation practices first came to the attention of the Western public and ideologies with themes of social, political and religious unity also arose.[7] Such cultural developments reflect stirrings in the collective imagination and point to the astrological meaning of Neptune, which became the ruling planet of Pisces in the modern era.[8] Neptune has the capacity to expand or alter states of awareness, the mind becoming fluid and receptive to impressions from what Jung called the collective unconscious,[9] and to the 'oceanic' feeling of being sublimely connected to everything.[10]

Sirens

One of the most powerful Neptunian experiences we can have is to fall madly in love with someone. When we experience the full immensity of romantic love, Venus reveals her exaltation in Pisces, where she abandons all to Neptune's waves. A love like this begins in the ocean, just like Aphrodite herself, born of the sea-foam. For such a love to ever become sustainable, it must weigh anchor, find dry land to survive, or else be forever tossed and thrown asunder by the unpredictable and all-devouring sea of longing. This directs us to the most Piscean of all mythic adventures, that of Odysseus. He is thwarted by the sea god he has offended as he strives to make his way home from the Trojan War. We could justifiably take the whole of *The Odyssey* as being reflective of Pisces, but one story stands out: his encounter with the Sirens. They are great enchantresses, with bird-like forms and beautiful female heads and faces. They create the sweetest, most divine music that even the strongest will cannot resist, and when sailors pass within earshot of their island they are invariably lured to their deaths. But Odysseus, wily Mercurial hero that he is (carrying strong Virgo medicine), enacts a cunning plan to avoid this fate. Having been forewarned, he blocks the ears of his crew with beeswax and instructs them to tie him to the ship's mast, insisting that they tighten his bonds whenever he begs to be released. Crucially, Odysseus does not block his own ears, for he longs to experience the painful but blissful longing that the Sirens' song inspires. He allows himself to be driven half-mad with desire, to surrender his mind to the divine muse. Odysseus is the most soulful of heroes, the one most prepared to sacrifice his own material ambition. Through the many trials that he faces on his journey home, he learns to surrender his male ego to the deep mysteries of the divine feminine.

The weaving and the unweaving

A lover will surrender themselves completely to love, and in becoming one with their beloved will experience a certain loss of identity. But if the threads that link them back to the soul are known to them, they will be smart enough to find themselves again. Odysseus is such a lover, and he is smart. His soul is leading him home, to his beloved Ithaca and his devoted wife, Penelope. We met her in Virgo, weaving her dress by day, and here we find her unweaving it by night in Pisces. I sometimes imagine her to be the architect of the entire Odyssey, weaving together Heaven and Earth, somehow conducting the cosmic pattern of events that guide her wayward husband's narrative. As Odysseus's extraordinary adventure unfolds it is the integrity and devotion of Penelope's weaving that gradually guides him home. Meanwhile, the unravelling chaos of her unweaving puts her in league with Poseidon and reflects the many twists and turns of the tale, through which Odysseus encounters powerful female characters who initiate him, teach him about love and loss and strip him of his pretences.

Making it sacred

Pisces is a sign of sacrifice, an uncomfortable idea to the modern way of thinking. Yet the root meaning of the word is *sacre facere*: 'to make sacred'. It points to something that is set apart from the mundane, given over to whatever spiritual power(s) we grant authority to. Blessing someone, leaving an offering, setting time aside to pray or meditate, putting someone else's interests before your own, participating in any ritual act dedicated to something greater-than-human: these are all forms of sacrifice. We know when we are involved in this type of dedication because it is not determined by our instinctive belly urge. When we make a sacrifice, we defer our desire for material gain or self-gratification, our need to look good or prove that we are right; we temporarily release our striving for worldly achievement and status. We surrender these preoccupations when we make a sacred offering, giving over the bread we made in Virgo for the sake of the soul.

Pisces medicine: compassion

Like all the water signs, Pisces stirs deep emotions, connecting us to the yearning or sorrowful aspect of the human condition. When we allow ourselves to actively grieve our losses, expressing them as art, poetry, music and ritual, our grief moves and transforms. It becomes a sacred act of compassion, for ourselves and for those we love, those we lose, those who hurt us and those we hurt. It begins with forgiveness, of ourselves and others, and it is entirely different from pity; it cuts much deeper into the soul. Pisces medicine reminds us that our joys and sorrows are connected. If two souls have been drawn together in a tryst of love or conflict, deep friendship or through a family bond, they are carried on the same current: finding each other, losing each other, finding each other again, like the two fishes forever tied by that silver thread of longing.

Compassion is the active encounter with suffering, and it

can only arise through a deep acknowledgement of what is shared between us. The word implies that we suffer together, and that we come together to passionately praise life. We have reached the last zodiac sign and so must love the end as we loved the beginning, be as willing to let go of the stuff of life as we were to seize hold of its arrival. It is said that the fertile, life-giving waters of the Nile were first filled with the tears of Isis as she wept for her murdered husband, Osiris.[11] When we hold space for our sorrows and walk together in our shared grief, what is revealed is our shared joy. When we surrender ourselves to the compassion that is present, there we will find grief and the praise of life dancing side by side in the deepest of our hearts, carried by the music of the wheel that turns within us, around us and beyond us.

The Pisces shadow: escapism

In 1846, the same year that Neptune was discovered, surgeon William Morton conducted the first successful public demonstration of anaesthesia used in a surgical operation. It is a marvellous historical synchrony, perfectly illustrative of that Neptunian/Piscean longing to be free of the pain of incarnation, with which we are most in touch in this sign. In this darkest hour before the dawn, when our faith is most severely tested, Pisces offers us ways of going through and ultimately transcending the pain, but also tempting ways out of it. We dance on the edge here. There is an episode in *The Odyssey* where Odysseus is aided in his transformation by the goddess-enchantress Circe, who acts as a kind of *initiatrix* figure for him. But at the point where he is perhaps about to have a huge breakthrough in understanding, he is seduced by one of her young nymphs, Calypso. For seven years, we are told, the hero forgets his mission, abandons his homeward journey, and becomes lost in his infatuation with Calypso, before Zeus finally breaks the enchantment.[12]

We find the same idea expressed in Martin Scorcese's controversial film, *The Last Temptation of Christ*. It is the moment where Christ pleads for mercy and is offered a way out of being crucified. He is taken down from the cross and allowed to experience the joy of sexual union and the chance to live out his days as an ordinary family man, freed of the suffering and resurrection that it is his destiny to experience. These are mythic examples of something we all face, the opportunity to escape from the painful longing of the soul to return home. Our culture provides us with all manner of anaesthesias, carrying the same promise: we won't have to fully face our own or another's pain, physical demise and inevitable death, won't have to experience our feelings of separation, isolation and disconnectedness. So we reach for the bottle, the dope, the antidepressant, the TV remote, idolising disembodied fantasies of redemption and salvation that tempt us to betray the soul's inevitable journey of transformation.

Too much or too little Pisces

If you have been served a high dose of Piscean medicine, you may feel somewhat removed from earthly reality, disinterested in the everyday stuff. You will tend to be empathic, highly sensitive to others' sorrows and joys and may, at times, struggle to distinguish them from your own. Your sympathies incline more towards the underdogs, the mystics, the artists, the disenfranchised and disadvantaged in society. You are devotional by nature and your heart will want to reach out in all directions and embrace it all. However, you may lack discernment at times and be easily influenced, rather susceptible to glamour, suspect gurus or ideologies. If so, you would do well to integrate the more discerning, grounding medicine of Virgo. Be like Odysseus in his encounter with the Sirens and create strong ritual containers for your otherworldly adventures.

If you don't have much access to this medicine, you may find it harder to let go and fear the loss of what you have. You might be more inclined to keep control of things, not let them get out of hand. You might fail to appreciate the interconnectedness of life in your need for clarity, definition and objectivity. You might tend to overlook the ambiguities, the mysteries, the poetry of life. You may want to consider practising what John Keats once called 'negative capability': that is, 'being in uncertainties, mysteries and doubts without any irritable reaching after fact and reason'.[13]

Bringing it all to the feet

During the Last Supper, when Christ announces his forthcoming fate, he interrupts the meal, places a towel around his waist and proceeds to wash the feet of his disciples. They are dumbstruck that their master should humble himself in this way and find it hard to accept at first; but the avatar of the Piscean Age assures them that they will come to understand why this is necessary, saying 'unless I wash your feet, you have no part of me'. He then goes on to instruct his twelve followers to wash each other's feet.[14] Pisces has rulership of the feet and this passage in John's gospel encodes the mystical relationship between the feet and the fishes, the sign of the embodiment of Christ. According to the original teachings of reflexology, there are twelve pathways or energy meridians through which qi (or chi) flows through the body from the head to the feet, from Aries to Pisces. Each pathway is connected with an organ system and they are arranged in six pairs. Here we have the zodiac laid out in the body, with its six pairs of opposing-complementary signs. By stimulating these pathways mapped in the soles of the feet, as initiating points for healing, practitioners claim that the energy flow in the body may be rebalanced.[15]

This sounds remarkably like what we have been doing here on this journey around the wheel, which has brought us from the head, with all its individualistic Arien drive and ambition, to the feet where we are humbled by the realisation of our connection to the whole. On the final day of the Pisces workshop on *The Alchemical Journey* each year, we invite participants to wash each other's feet, in honour of the pilgrimage we have taken together. Feeling into the profound sensitivity of that experience, we begin to remember that there is no separation. Everything is connected. We are one with each other, one with Mother Earth, one with all the beings that are held within her compassionate embrace.

Pisces summary

Spend time during this twelfth and final stage of the wheel contemplating your relationship to endings and notice how able you are to let go. Feel into the love and compassion at the very heart of your being. Work with the following enquiries and suggested activities. Write down your thoughts, feelings and responses in your journal, and be prepared to really examine yourself through this medicine.

CONSIDER THESE QUESTIONS, ASK YOURSELF:

- What am I holding on to that is causing me to suffer?

- What am I struggling to accept in myself and in others?

- What means do I use to escape, to avoid facing the end of things?

- Who in my life do I need to forgive?

- What do I need to grieve?

- In what ways could I praise life more than I do?

- In what areas of my life do I need to cultivate compassion?

SUGGESTED PRACTICES AND ACTIVITIES

- 'Let Go, Let God': Imagine something in your life that you are holding that is a source of fear, pain, anger or resentment. Spend time in meditation; picture yourself

holding whatever it is tightly in your grip; acknowledge it and bless it, then simply and gently release
your grip on it and allow it go where it needs to go,
with your blessing.

- Practise compassion for those around you, both living
  and dead, especially those with whom you experience
  a strong emotional tug. Imagine yourselves tied like
  the fishes, remembering that even when you are
  pulling in different directions, your souls are forever
  connected and partake of the same longing.

- Spend time connecting with your feet. Consider
  having a relaxing foot massage or reflexology session,
  and meditate upon the twelve zodiacal meridians of
  energy within your body.

- Spend time contemplating the journey you have taken
  around the wheel, the twelve medicines you have
  encountered along the way, the realisations that you
  have had; consider any ways in which you see your
  life differently as a result. Spend some time writing
  down your insights in your journal.

Completing the wheel

Full circle

So you have come full circle. Think about the journey you have taken here. In what ways has it opened your imagination to enquire into the different aspects of your life? Through your adventure around the wheel you have been invited to enquire into twelve distinct perspectives on the world, each rich in story and symbolism. These have been revealed as twelve essential modalities of a comprehensive self-development cycle, twelve vital stages in a process of initiation towards becoming a complete human being. You have encountered twelve members of your personal assembly, seated in order at the round table of your astrological imagination. They are ready to work with you now to restore trust, integrity and natural abundance to your life, to help you realise the potential you were born to manifest. So how do you feel now? What have you learned? Do you view your life differently? Have you been prompted to make changes in your life? How do you see your future?

The food of the soul

A deep study of the zodiac wheel helps restore associations between things that we have forgotten are connected. It shows us how they constellate around the particular archetypal images of the astrological signs, how those images are woven into the fabric of our natural, cultural and spiritual understanding. James Hillman reminds us that the soul is 'not a substance, but a set of perspectives ... a mode that recognises all realities as primarily symbolic or metaphorical'.[1] Enriching one's astrological imagination can help us not to take our suffering so literally; to have whatever ails us remembered as the story, image or symbol that it primarily is. By recalling the mythic component that permeates all the circumstances of our lives and underpins all our psychological reasoning, by honouring myth as the food of the soul, we can address our deepest wounds and undertake the path of healing and restoration for which we all long.

In the end is our beginning

The end of the cycle returns us to its beginning and we can see that beginning with new eyes. Often the treasure we seek in life is right under our noses, but until we have taken the adventure we are unable to appreciate that it is so. There is something reassuring about returning home; but when we have endured the tests and trials to which any conscious journey will subject us, we cannot help but see home differently. In the words of T.S. Eliot, 'We shall not cease from exploration, and the end of all our exploring will be to arrive where we started and know the place for the first time.'[2] We are not just going in circles; we are evolving our consciousness, opening up new possibilities for expression, becoming more aware of our imbalances and empowering our choices in life. The zodiac is inherently multi-layered; each time we engage consciously with the turning wheel we can integrate more refined, more subtle aspects of each medicine. The next time you read this book you will read it differently, make new associations and have fresh insights. Journeying in the wheel thus becomes a spiral. Just as our planet traces out a spiral-like helix pattern in space as our sun orbits the centre of the galaxy, so our consciousness spirals with each turning of our internal zodiac wheel.[3] And that spiralling, evolutionary impulse reaches in two directions: upwards through the medium of air towards the fire of spirit, and downwards through the containment of earth into the deep water of soul.

The transition from Pisces to Aries

When Christ told his disciples that he was the alpha and the omega, the first and the last, he alluded to the mystery of this final, most profound transition in the wheel.[4] Only through the dissolution of our personally identified sense of self in Pisces may we find ourselves born again in Aries. But how much do we remember as we pass this threshold? The ancients spoke of the river of forgetfulness, Lethe, one of the five great rivers of the Underworld.[5] As souls entered incarnation, they were offered a draught of its waters to drink, and only the wisest few could resist. So the vast majority of us enter this world with no recollection of the long journey that our soul has travelled to be here, oblivious to our karma, unable to remember the purpose behind our incarnation, or even that there is one. As we enter Aries, we awake abruptly from our slumber, must suddenly let go of what has gone before, as the onset of birth prompts us to be alive and present. Memory is lost in the great enthusiasm of the moment. Nature has designed it that way. The memory of our soul's journey can be recovered and the wisdom inherent in the zodiac wheel points the way. The alchemists of old often wore a Phrygian or Mithraic cap, which flopped over like a fish pointing to the feet; it was a secret sign that they had been initiated into the zodiacal mysteries.[6] Wearing a fish on your head connects Pisces to Aries, the feet to the head, omega to alpha, the end to the beginning. We have a tradition on *The Alchemical Journey* of awarding a specially made Mithraic cap to those who complete the whole zodiacal round.

The journey continues ...

I encourage you to re-read this book and keep working with the exercises. Let the stories, images and poetry claim some part of you. It takes time and space for any medicine to work, so relax your rational mind as best you can; there is no need to analyse or understand exactly what is going on. Now that you have integrated each zodiacal perspective in order, you are well resourced to draw on their respective teachings as and when you need them and now, being alert to the rich tapestry of synchronicity in your life, you are able to discern which zodiac image is showing itself at any given time. The more you engage with the zodiac, the more wonders it will reveal. To paraphrase the seventeenth-century Christian mystic Jakob Böhme, the essence of God is like a wheel; the more one looks at it, the more one learns about its form, the greater longing one has towards it, and the greater pleasure one has in the wheel.[7] Enjoy the journey!

Endnotes

Introduction

1 This is a circular figure that plots the positions of the Sun, Moon and planets at the moment of your birth against the backdrop of the twelve zodiac signs.

2 This began as a twelve-week course, initially called 'Living a Wealthy Life' and it produced remarkable shifts in people's lives. The Alchemical Journey is a year-long course that has been running in Glastonbury, UK, since 2010. It includes monthly pilgrimages into Glastonbury's landscape zodiac 'Temple of the Stars' as part of the programme. This zodiac is comprised of a complete circle of landscape effigies, eleven miles in diameter, that appear in the Somerset countryside. It was perceived in the 1920s by a local artist and esotericist, Katharine Maltwood. While studying local maps, she began to see astrological figures marked out by rivers, old trackways, field boundaries and the contours of certain hills. These forays into Glastonbury's symbolic landscape offer up an intricate tapestry of meaningful and revealing synchronicities.

3 We can also observe a thirteenth constellation, Ophiuchus, lying between Scorpio and Sagittarius, which partially intrudes into the elegant twelve-fold symmetry of the zodiacal ecliptic. See the Scorpio chapter for more information.

4 There is a distinction to be made between the twelve constellations of the ecliptic and the zodiac signs that derive their names from them. Western and Indian astrologers use a differently aligned zodiac. In the West, we use the *tropical zodiac*, which means that the first degree of the sign Aries is tied to the Spring Equinox, where it was originally conceived to be, Cancer to Summer Solstice, Libra to Autumn Equinox and Capricorn to Winter Solstice, with each sign being allotted a 30-degree segment within the 360-degree wheel. This was established by Ptolemy in his Tetrabiblos. See: http://www.sacred-texts.com/astro/ptb/ptb15.htm – accessed 9 July 17. However, due to a phenomenon called the precession of the equinoxes, the ecliptic circle of stars gradually shifts in its orientation to the solstices and equinoxes, to the extent of one degree of longitude roughly every 72 years, so the actual constellations have shifted. Indian astrology works with the *sidereal zodiac* and takes this precessional shift into account, which better preserves the relationship between star constellation and sign, but loses the original seasonal reference points, which don't change. This precessional shift was known about in the West, but because the zodiac was such an important calendrical device, the zodiac signs were held fixed

to the seasonal markers. The sign that is rising at Spring Equinox marks the Astrological Age. These gradually slip backwards through the zodiacal constellations, and we are currently on the cusp between Pisces and Aquarius.

5 For discussion of this, see Roy Willis and Patrick Curry, *Astrology, Science & Culture: Pulling Down the Moon* (New York: Berg, 2004), pp. 1–14.

6 Stanslas Klossowski de Rola, *Alchemy: The Secret Art* (New York: Bounty Books, 1973), p. 7.

7 Noel Cobb, foreword to: Thomas Moore, *The Planets Within: The Astrological Psychology of Marsilio Ficino* (Maryland: Lindisfarne Books, 1989), p. 12.

8 For discussion of how the zodiac was incorporated into Mithraism, see for example: Roger Beck, *The Religion of the Mithras Cult in the Empire: Mysteries of the Unconquered Sun* (Oxford: Oxford University Press, 2006).

9 See earlier note 4.

10 Jung, Carl Gustav, 'Letter to André Barbault, 26 May 1954' in *Letters* (London: Routledge & Kegan Paul, 1954), p. 177.

11 Mircea Eliade, *The Myth of the Eternal Return* (New York: Princeton University Press, 2005).

12 C.G. Jung, 'Foreword to the I-Ching', at http://members.aol.com/iching64/jung.htm.

13 Carl Sagan, *The Dragons of Eden: Speculations on the Evolution of Human Intelligence* (New York: Ballantine Books, 1986).

14 Plato, *Timaeus [55c]*, cited by James Hillman in article entitled: 'Heaven Retains Within its Sphere Half of All Bodies and Maladies' (1997), http://www.springpub.com/astro.htm.

15 John Michell and Christine Rhone, *Twelve Tribe Nations and the Science of Enchanting the Landscape* (Grand Rapids, MI: Phanes Press, 1991), p. 74.

16 Ibid., p. 92.

17 Vicki Burke, *The Journey to the Golden City: Finding the Way Home* (Leicester: Matador, 2017).

The First Gateway: Aries

1 See Darby Costello, 'Desire and the Stars', published in *Astrological Journal* vol. 45 (July/August 2003).

2 Robert Graves, *The Greek Myths* Vol. I (Pennsylvania: Folio Society, 2005), p. 216.

3 Emmeline Plunkett, *Calendars & Constellations of the Ancient World* (New York: Cosimo Classics, 2005), pp. 18, 33–34.

4 This marks the time of 'passing over', referring to the tenth plague that all the first-born male children would perish at the hand of God, except for those of the 'true faith' who had marked their doorposts with a ram's/lamb's blood.

5 Nicholas Campion, *The Dawn of Astrology: A Cultural History of Western Astrology* (London: Hambledon Continuum, 2008), p. 114.

6 Dorsha Hayes, 'Fire Hazard', cited by Barbara Somers, *Fires of Alchemy: A Transpersonal Viewpoint* (Shaftesbury: Archive, 2004), pp. 68–69.

7 See: http://www.trogironline.com/history_culture/kairos.html.

8 Robert Graves, *The Greek Myths* (Pennsylvania: Folio Society, 2005), pp. 34–38.

9 Emblem VIII from Michael Meyer's *Atalanta Fugiens*. The epigram attached
   to the image reads: 'There is a bird, the most sublime of all / To find whose
   egg should be your only care / Its white surround a soft and golden yolk: /
   one cautiously attacks with fiery sword / Let Vulcan aid the work of Mars:
   / the chick hatched thence will conquer / both the iron and the fire.' H. M.
   E. de Jong, *Michael Maier's Atalanta Fugiens: Sources of an Alchemical Book of
   Emblems* (Berwick, ME: Nicolas-Hays Inc, 2002), epigram 8. To see the image,
   visit http://commons.wikimedia.org/wiki/File:Michael_Maier_Atalanta_
   Fugiens_Emblem_08.jpeg

The Second Gateway: Taurus

1 http://treesforlife.org.uk/forest/mythology-folklore/hawthorn/ – accessed
   19 June 2017.
2 http://www.darkdorset.co.uk/the_maypole – accessed on 19 June 2017.
3 Pamela Coleman Smith and Arthur Edward Waite, *The Rider Tarot Deck:
   Known also as the Waite Tarot and the Rider-Waite Tarot* (Stamford: U.S. Games
   Systems, 1971).
4 Lynne Twist, *The Soul of Money* (New York: Norton, 2003), pp. 49–50.
5 Ibid., p. 47.
6 Robert Graves, *The Greek Myths* Vol. I (Pennsylvania: Folio Society, 2005),
   pp. 274–275.
7 Robert Graves, *The Greek Myths* Vol. II (Pennsylvania: Folio Society, 2005),
   section 129.
8 http://www.religionfacts.com/laughing-buddha – accessed on 19 June 2017
9 Twist, *Soul of Money*, p. 97.
10 James Hillman, *A Blue Fire* (New York: Harper Perennial, 1989), p. 174.

The Third Gateway: Gemini

1 I had this experience in Cape Town in 2007, when a friend innocently
   admired the brooch of a *sangoma* diviner. He immediately offered it to her
   and, to her great embarrassment, she had no choice but to accept it!
2 King James Bible, Acts 2: (1–31) https://www.kingjamesbibleonline.org/
   Acts-Chapter-2/ – accessed on 26 June 2017.
3 Patrick Harpur, *The Philosopher's Secret Fire: A History of the Imagination*
   (Michigan: Penguin, 2002), pp. 264–5.
4 See: Lewis Hyde, *Trickster Makes this World: How Disruptive Imagination Creates
   Culture* (Edinburgh: Canongate, 2008). pp. 55–80.
5 Ibid., pp. 58–59.
6 Jonathan Gotschall, *The Storytelling Animal: How Stories Make us Human*
   (Wilmington, MA: Mariner Books, 2003), p. 161.
7 David Abram, *The Spell of the Sensuous: Perception and Language in a More-
   Than-Human World* (New York: Vintage, 1997), p.130.
8 Harpur, *Philosopher's Secret Fire*, p. 209.
9 Abram, *Spell of the Sensuous*, p. 238.

The Fourth Gateway: Cancer

1 Abram, *Spell of the Sensuous*. p. 89.
2 Marsilio Ficino (trans. Michael J. Allen), *Platonic Theology, Vol. 6, Books 17–18* (Cambridge, MA: Harvard University Press, 2006), p. 113.
3 This is directly opposite the birthday of Christ in the calendar, six months after Winter Solstice, which is associated with the ascent of the Sun, being the portal through which the avatar of the age is said to incarnate. Christ shares his birthday with Mithras, avatar of the Roman mystery tradition. More on that in the Capricorn chapter.
4 Ronald Hutton, *The Stations of the Sun: A History of the Ritual Year in Britain* (Oxford: Oxford University Press, 1996), p. 311.
5 http://www.theoi.com/Ther/Karkinos.html – accessed on 20 July 2017.
6 Hera placed a curse on Alcmene, Heracles's mother, delaying his birth in a jealous act of revenge against his father, Zeus. Hera becomes his foster mother and, having driven him mad as an adult, causes him to slaughter his wife and family. By way of atonement, she sets him to his twelve gruelling labours. See, for example: Ted Hughes, *Tales from Ovid* (London: Faber & Faber, 1997), pp. 164–167.
7 Hathor is often depicted as a cow, feeding the young pharaoh from her milk.
8 Jonathon Amos, 'Dung beetles guided by Milky Way' at: http://www.bbc.com/news/science-environment-21150721 – accessed on 5 May 2017.
9 Thomas Moore, *The Re-Enchantment of Everyday Life* (New York: Harper Perennial, 1997), pp. 41–42.
10 Harpur, *Philosopher's Secret Fire*. p. 217.
11 Ibid., p. 217.
12 Michael A. Sells, *Mystical Languages of Unsaying* (Chicago: University of Chicago Press), p. 31.
13 Prudence Jones (ed.), *Creative Astrology, Experiential Understanding in the Horoscope* (London: Aquarian, 1991), p. 1.

The Fifth Gateway: Leo

1 The Sun is exalted in the sign of Aries.
2 See for example: Patricia Monaghan (ed.), *Goddesses in World Culture: Vol. I, Asia & Africa* (Santa Barbara, CA: Praeger, 2011), p. 259.
3 See for example: Rachel Alexander, *Myths, Symbols and Legends of Solar System Bodies* (New York: Springer, 2015), p. 9.
4 Patricia Monaghan (ed.), *Goddesses*, p. 208.
5 Lindsay River and Sally Gillespie, *The Knot of Time: Astrology & Female Experience* (St Paul, MN: Women's Press, 1997).
6 *Rider-Waite Tarot*.
7 Robert Graves, *The Greek Myths* (Manchester: Carcanet Press Ltd, 2001), pp. 465–475.
8 Odysseus, by contrast, is a master of wit and subtlety, and engages deeply with death and with the dark feminine, Hillman identifies him as a hero of the soul. We will meet him properly in the water sign, Pisces. See: James Hillman, *The Dream and the Underworld* (New York: Harper & Row, 1979), p. 110.

9 Ibid., p. 110.
10 Arnold van Gennep, *The Rites of Passage* (London & New York: Routledge, 2010).
11 Marianne Williamson, *A Return to Love: Reflections on the Principles of 'A Course in Miracles'* (New York: Harper Collins, 1992), pp. 191–192.

The Sixth Gateway: Virgo

1 Margeurite Rigoglioso, *The Cult of Divine Birth in Ancient Greece* (New York: Macmillan, 2009), pp. 1–3.
2 See for example: http://www.stellarhousepublishing.com/anahita.pdf.
3 See for example: R. Gordon Wasson, Albert Hofmann and Carla P. Ruck, *The Road to Eleusis: Unveiling the Secret of the Mysteries* (Berkeley, CA: North Atlantic Books, 2008).
4 http://www.theoi.com/Olympios/AthenaMyths.html.
5 Robert Graves, *The Greek Myths* (Manchester: Carcanet Press Ltd. 2001) p. 732.
6 See for example: René Devisch, *Weaving the Threads of Life, The Khita Gyn-Eco-Logical Healing Cult Among the Yaka* (Chicago: University of Chicago Press, 1993), p.160; Kathy M'Closkey, *Swept Under the Rug: A Hidden History of Navajo Weaving* (Albuquerque, NM: University of New Mexico Press, 2002), pp. 15–23.
7 Jacob Ludwig Carl Grimm, *Teutonic Mythology* (Mineola, NY: Dover Phoenix, 2004 [1882]), p. 426.
8 Alby Stone, *Wyrd: Fate and Destiny in North European Paganism*, (self-published, 1989), pp. 22–23.
9 Ibid.

The Seventh Gateway: Libra

1 Geraldine Thorston, *The Goddess in Your Stars* (New York: Simon & Schuster, 1989), p. 108.
2 Karl Kerenyi, *The Gods of the Greeks* (London and New York: Thames and Hudson, 1951), pp. 105–106.
3 https://www.britannica.com/topic/Michaelmas.
4 C.G. Jung, *Collected Works Vol. 9: Aieon* (Princeton, OR: Princeton University Press, 1981), p. 126.
5 This link between Libra and Tiresias is made by Liz Greene. See Liz Greene, *Astrology for Lovers* (San Francisco, CA: Weiser, 1989), p. 259.
6 Jonathan Annas and Julia Barnes, *Sextus Empiricus' Outlines of Pyrrhonism* (Cambridge: Cambridge Univeristy Press, 2002).
7 Jelaluddin Rumi, *The Essential Rumi*, transl. Coleman Barks (New Jersey: Castle Books, 1997), p.36.
8 Robert Graves, *The Greek Myths* (Manchester: Carcanet Press Ltd, 2001), pp. 632–633.
9 Kerenyi, *Gods of the Greeks*, pp. 105–106
10 An inferior conjunction occurs when Venus is on the Earth's side of the Sun in the same degree of the zodiac, and a superior conjunction when it is on the far side of the Sun from Earth.
11 John Martineau, *A Little Book of Coincidence in the Solar System* (Glastonbury: Wooden Books, 2001), pp. 24–26.

The Eighth Gateway: Scorpio

1 Antonio Machado (trans. Robert Bly), *Times Alone: Selected Poems of Antonio Machado* (Middletown, CT: Wesleyan; Bilingual Spanish-English edn 1983), p. 105.
2 In earlier times, the Scorpius constellation was larger and contained the stars of Libra, cited in Ptolemy's *Tetrabiblos* as the Claws of the Scorpion. In its reduced form, it only occupies nine degrees of the zodiacal band, and the Sun only spends nine days travelling through its stars. The other twenty-one days of the Sun's passage through this segment of the heavens are claimed by the group of stars known as Ophiuchus, the Serpent Bearer, the so-called 'thirteenth sign'. So it testifies to the prevailing impact of the scorpion in the human imagination that it has retained its symbolic place in the zodiacal round.
3 The Virgo glyph also contains the harvesting sickle.
4 See: Margaret Starbird, *The Woman with the Alabaster Jar: Mary Magdalen and the Holy Grail* (Rochester, VT: Bear & Co, 1993), p. xix.
5 Ibid.
6 Richard Allen, *Star Names: Their Lore and Meaning* (New York: Dover, 1963), p. 305.
7 Allen, *Star Names*, p. 308; Bernadette Brady, *Brady's Book of Fixed Stars* (York, ME: Weiser, 1998), pp. 163–65.
8 See for example, Elisabeth Haich, *Initiation* (Santa Fe, NM: Aurora Press, 2000), p. 246. Scorpio is associated with an eagle in the Book of Revelation, and biblical prophet Ezekiel described a vision, believed to be drawn from Babylonian astrology, which includes an eagle representing Scorpio on the 'fixed cross of matter'. These four signs also become associated with the four evangelists, or gospel writers, with the Scorpio eagle being John.
9 The other royal stars are Aldebaran (in Taurus), Regulus (in Leo) and Formalhaut (in Piscis Australis, below Aquarius). Each is found in the constellations of the four fixed zodiac signs, and is known as the fixed star cross.
10 'Poppy', https://b-and-t-world-seeds.com/Poppya.htm – accessed 24 June 2017.
11 It is interesting to note that the poppy is a companion plant of wheat and barley, the grains which Demeter granted as gifts to humans.
12 See for example: Alan F. Alford, *The Midnight Sun: The Death and Rebirth of God in Ancient Egypt* (Walsall: Eridu Books, 2004).
13 See for example: Stanton Marlan, *The Dark Sun, the Alchemy & Art of Darkness* (Texas A&M University Press, 2005).
14 Peter Kingsley, *In the Dark Places of Wisdom*, (Inverness, CA: Golden Sufi Centre, 1999), p. 63.
15 Robert Bly, *A Little Book on the Shadow* (New York: Harper Collins, 1988).
16 Robert Bly, *Stealing Sugar From the Castle*, Selected and New Poems, 1950–2013 (W.W. Norton, 2013), p.3.

The Ninth Gateway: Sagittarius

1 Lee Billings, 'Jupiter, Destroyer of Worlds, May Have Paved the Way for Earth', in *Scientific American*, 1 April 2015; Deborah Byrd, 'Is it true that Jupiter protects Earth?', http://earthsky.org/space/is-it-true-that-jupiter-protects-earth.

2 *The Mystical Hymns of Orpheus,* trans. by Th. Taylor (London, 1846).

3 Astrologers tend to engage with Chiron primarily through the tiny planet-like body of that name orbiting erratically from within the bounds of Saturn to beyond the reach of Uranus. Discovered in 1977, it excited the astrologer's imagination when it was named after this charismatic horse-man, the emphasis being placed primarily upon his role as the wounded healer or shaman. See: Melanie Reinhart, *Chiron: The Wounded Healer* (London: Penguin, 1990).

4 We end up with a centaur, despite the fact that (it is said) Zeus was unable to displace Crotus from his place on the ecliptic, and was instead forced to place Chiron further south in the constellation of Centaurus, which is never seen in the northern hemisphere. See: Bernadette Brady, *Brady's Book of Fixed Stars* (Boston, MA: Weiser, 1998).

5 Janet Farrah and Virginia Russell, *The Magical History of the Horse* (London: Robert Hale, 1992), pp. 53–55.

6 Mircea Eliade, *Shamanism: Archaic Techniques of Ecstacy* (London: Routledge, 1964), pp. 467–470.

7 Melanie Reinhart, *Chiron: The Wounded Healer* (London: Penguin, 1990), p. 19.

8 Ibid.

9 http://www.theoi.com/Georgikos/KentaurosKheiron.html.

10 William Blake, *On the Marriage of Heaven and Hell* (Oxford: Oxford University Press, 1975).

11 Frederich Nietzsche [1879], *The Birth of Tragedy* (Penguin Classics, 2003).

12 Abaris, a priest of Apollo, flies on this arrow, 'as on a witch's broomstick'. See Mircea Eliade, *Shamanism,* pp. 387–389. See also: John Wood [1765], *A Description of Bath* (Bath: Kingsmead Reprints, 1969), pp. 33–38. Citing: Diodorus Siculus, Book II, http://penelope.uchicago.edu/Thayer/E/Roman/Texts/Diodorus_Siculus/2B*.html.

13 Manilius, *Astronomica* II. 433–438, cited by Charlotte R. Long, *The Twelve Gods of Greece and Rome* (Leiden, NL: E.J. Brill, 1987), pp. 109–110.

14 Graves, *The Greek Myths,* pp. 84–85.

15 A. T. Mann, *A New Vision of Astrology: From Conception to Transcendence* (New York: Pocket Books, 2002), p. 47.

The Tenth Gateway: Capricorn

1 Victor Frankl [1946], *Man's Search for Meaning* (Boston, MA: Beacon Press, 2006), p. 108.

2 See for example: Frederick H. Borsch, *The Son of Man in Myth and History* (Eugene, OR: Wipf & Stock, 2007) , pp. 96–99.

3 Rupert Gleadlow, *The Origin of the Zodiac* (New York: Dover Publications, 2011), p. 166; *The Zodiac Revealed* (Hollywood, CA: Wilshire, 1972), pp. 126–27.

4 See for example: Lesley Bushnell, 'The Wild Goat-and-Tree Icon and its Special Significance for Ancient Cyprus', in Proceedings of Cypriot Archaeology Conference Papers, 2005. https://www.academia.edu/5171719/The_wild_goat_and_tree_icon_and_its_special_significance_for_Cyprus – accessed on 8 July 2017.

5 Marsilio Ficino, *Platonic Theology, Vol. 6, Books 17–18*, p. 113. Also: Alice A. Bailey, *Esoteric Astrology* (London: Lucis Trust, 1979), pp. 153–174.

6 Jacob Bar-Salabi, cited in Ramsay MacMullen, *Christianity and Paganism in the Fourth to Eighth Centuries* (New Haven, CT: Yale University Press, 1997), p. 155.

7 It is often stated that the avatar of the Roman mystery cult, Mithra, whose stock epithet was *sol invictus*, was also born on 25th December, and this would fit the pattern that emerges through the symbolism, though the actual evidence for this is disputed. For discussion see Roger Beck, 'Merkelbach's Mithras' in *Phoenix* vol. 41 no. 3 (Autumn 1987): 296–316. Accessed via: https://www.jstor.org/stable/1088197.

8 I was privileged to be present at Taunton Museum with my colleague Anthony Thorley for the unveiling of a rare and perfectly preserved bronze goat-fish, found in Somerset's Mendip Hills in south-west England. Dated to the second century CE, this would have belonged to a member of a Roman legion, and would have symbolised the Roman Emperor at the time, a statement of his credentials as supreme leader, sanctioned by the authority of the Unconquerable Sun.

9 The ritual driving-out of a she-goat beyond the bounds of society is also attested in Syria upon the coronation of a king during 'elimination rites' that were supposed to help purify the community of its evils.

10 http://www.theoi.com/Georgikos/Pan.html – accessed on 26 June 2017.

11 Percy Bysshe Shelley, 'Hymn of Pan': https://www.poetryfoundation.org/poems-and-poets/poems/detail/45122 – accessed on 26 June 2017.

12 John Keats, 'Hymn to Pan': http://www.bartleby.com/333/348.html – accessed on 26 June 2107.

13 'The Piper at the Gates of Dawn' is the title of one of the chapters in Kenneth Grahame's *Wind in the Willows* and in the book, the characters visit the Holy Island of Pan. See: Kenneth Grahame, *The Wind in the Willows* (Ware: Wordsworth Classics, 1993), pp. 97–108. This epithet was taken up by songwriter Syd Barrett, and became the title of Pink Floyd's first album.

14 William Blake, 'The Marriage of Heaven and Hell', quoted in Elizabeth M. Knowles (ed.), *Oxford Dictionary of Quotations* (Oxford: Oxford University Press, 1999), p. 119.

15 Amalthea was placed among the stars as the constellation Capra (sometimes confused with Capricorn), the stellar group surrounding Capella, often called 'the goat star', on the arm of the Auriga constellation, who is often depicted as a goatherd or shepherd.

16 G. Ronald Murphy, SJ, *Tree of Salvation: Yggdrasil and the Cross in the North* (Oxford: Oxford University Press, 2013), pp. 5–6.

17 Giorgio de Santillana and Hertha von Dechend, *Hamlet's Mill: An Essay on Myth and the Frame of Time* (Boston: Nonpareil Books, 1977), p. 3. Cited by Bernadette Brady, *Brady's Book of Fixed Stars* (Boston, MA: Weiser, 1998), p. 1.

18 Brady, *Book of Fixed Stars*, p. 1.

19 1 January was consecrated to Janus, and the month of January named after him. See: https://romanpagan.wordpress.com/janus/ – citing Ovid, *Fasti*, 1 January. Accessed on 26 July 2017.

20 This is reflective of Saturn's exaltation in the sign of Libra.

The Eleventh Gateway: Aquarius

1 'I am a river to my people', from the film *Lawrence of Arabia*.
2 The month of February is named after *Februa*, a rite of cleansing and purification conducted in Roman times, in preparation for a new beginning, the inauguration of spring. See: https://en.wikipedia.org/wiki/Lupercalia – accessed on 27 June 2017.
3 Patricia Monaghan, *The Goddess Path: Myths, Invocations & Rituals* (St. Paul, MN: Llewellyn, 2004), pp. 173–174.
4 http://www.egyptianmyths.net/hapi.htm.
5 Sirius was known to the Egyptians as Sodpet, and to the Greeks as Sothis, and this was commonly conflated with Isis. See for example: http://www.mirrorofisis.freeyellow.com/id63.html.
6 See for example: Cyril Fagan, *Astrological Origins* (St Paul, MN: Llewellyn, 1971), p. 109.
7 Brady, *Book of Fixed Stars*, p. 308.
8 See: Rabbi Joel C. Dobin, *Kabbalistic Astrology: The Sacred Tradition of the Hebrew Sages* (Rochester, VE: Inner Tradtions International, 1999), p. 109.
9 Ibid.
10 *Samson and Delilah*, by Andrea Mantegna in the National Gallery in London.
11 Like Hapi, Ganymede is a sexually ambiguous character and has become a modern-day icon among the gay community. See for example: Robert Aldrich and Garry Wotherspoon (eds.) *Who's Who in Gay & Lesbian History* (Routledge, 2002), pp. 205–206.
12 River and Gillespie, *The Knot of Time*, p. 203.
13 Fritjof Capra, *The Turning Point: Science, Society and the Rising Culture* (New York: Simon & Schuster, 1982), p. 290.
14 This did not occur until the nineteenth century and really did not establish itself fully until the development of a more psychological astrology in the twentieth century. For discussion, see: Kim Farnell, *When and why did Uranus become associated with Aquarius?* – http://www.skyscript.co.uk/ur_aq.html.
15 Peter Kalkavage (ed.), *Plato's Timaeus* (Indiana, IN: Hackett Publishing, 2001), 54E–55C; pp. 88–89.
16 Richard Tarnas, *Cosmos and Psyche* (New York: Plume, 2007).
17 Prometheus was bound to a rock in the Underworld, where each day a vulture would peck out his liver, which would then grow back again each night, causing him eternal suffering. He was eventually freed from this fate when the wise and kindly centaur, Chiron, offered to exchange places with him in order to be able to die there and relieve his own immortal suffering.
18 See: Israel Regardie, *The Golden Dawn: An Account of the Teachings, Rites and Ceremonies of the Order of the Golden Dawn* (Woodbury, MN: Llewellyn Worldwide, 2016).
19 Coleman Smith and Arthur Edward Waite, *The Rider Tarot*.
20 Alesteir Crowley, *The Book of Thoth Tarot* (Newburyport, MA: Red Wheel / Weiser, 1981).
21 Juliet Sharman-Burke and Liz Greene, *The Mythic Tarot* (London: Rider, 1989).
22 Graves, *The Greek Myths*, p. 145.
23 Ibid., pp. 711–713.

24 Gail Thomas, *Healing Pandora: The Restoration of Hope and Abundance* (Berkeley, CA: North Atlantic Books, 2009), p. xv.

The Twelfth Gateway: Pisces

1 Albert Einstein, *Einstein on Cosmic Religion and Other Opinions and Aphorisms* (Mineola, NY: Dover Publications, 2009), p. 97.
2 A significant conjunction of Jupiter and Saturn closely aligned with *Al Rescha* in 7 BCE. Astrologers at the time, aware that the vernal equinox point was slipping from Aries to Pisces, would have looked east to the stars of the fishes for a sign of celestial inspiration, expectant of an avatar who might bind humanity in peace and unity. When this star featured strongly in a person's birthchart, it was said to indicate someone 'prone to exploration of extremes and sympathy for opposing viewpoints'. See Deborah Houlding, *Star Lore of the Constellations: Pisces, The Fishes,* http://www.skyscript.co.uk/pisces_myth.html.
3 See for example: http://www.jesuswalk.com/christian-symbols/early-christian-symbols.htm.
4 The Gospel According to Matthew, 4:19. https://www.kingjamesbibleonline. org/ – accessed on 27 June 2017.
5 James Hillman, *Re-Visioning Psychology* (New York: Harper Perennial, 1992), p. xvi.
6 See for example: Peter Hay, *Main Currents in Western Environmental Thought* (Indianapolis, IN: Indiana University Press, 2002), p. 5.
7 Communism, the labour movement and Unitarianism, among others.
8 The constellation of Pisces had already been under the care of this god of the sea since the early days of astrology, as in the *Neptune Sidus* of Manilius. See: Allen, *Star Names*, p. 340.
9 See, for example: http://www.carl-jung.net/collective_unconscious.html – accessed on 27 June 2017.
10 Psychotherapists sometimes refer to the 'oceanic feeling' that patients report as an undifferentiated state of at-oneness with the Universe, either as Freud suggests as a 'primitive-ego-feeling' recalled from infancy where the child has not yet distinguished himself as being different from his surroundings, or as the basis of valid religious experience, some form of mystical union with the divine. For discussion, see: Jean-Michel Quinodoz (trans. David Alcorn), *Reading Freud: A Chronological Exploration of Freud's Writings* (London and New York: Routledge, 2004), p. 237.
11 R.E. Witt, *Isis in the Ancient World* (Ithaca: NY, Cornell University Press, 1971), p. 166.
12 Homer, *The Odyssey* Vol. I (Boston, MA: Osgood & Co., 1871) p. 211. See also Lindsay Clarke's insightful rendering of the story: *The Return from Troy* (London: HarperCollins, 2006), pp. 369–370.
13 Anon. 'Keats's Negative Capability' (text of personal letter written in 1817): URL = http://www.mrbauld.com/negcap.html accessed on 8 July 2017.
14 John 13:1–17. https://www.kingjamesbibleonline.org/John-Chapter-13/ – accessed on 8 July 2017
15 Beryl Crane, *Reflexology: The Definitive Practitioner's Manual* (HarperCollins UK, 2012).

Completing the Wheel

1 Hillman, *Re-visioning Psychology*, p. x.
2 T.S. Eliot, 'Little Gidding', from *The Four Quartets*. See for example: Sunil Kumar Sarker, *T.S. Eliot: Poetry, Plays & Prose* (New Delhi: India, Atlantic Publishers & Dist, 2007), p. 154.
3 See: A .T. Mann, *Astrology and the Art of Healing* (New York, NY: Paraview, 2004), p. 37.
4 The Book of Revelation, 22:13. https://www.kingjamesbibleonline.org/ Revelation-22-13/ – accessed on 27 July 2017.
5 Edith Hamilton, *Mythology: Timeless Tales of Gods and Heroes*, (London: Penguin, 1969, pp. 39, 228.
6 David Ovason, *The Zelator: A Modern Initiate Explore the Ancient Mysteries* (Newburyport, MA: Weiser, 2000), p. 317.
7 *Confessions of Jakob Bohme*, pp. 41–42. https://archive.org/stream/ confessionsofjac00bohmiala/confessionsofjac00bohmiala_djvu.txt – accessed on 27 June 2017.

Bibliography

Abram, David, *The Spell of the Sensuous: Perception and Language in a More-Than-Human World* (New York: Vintage, 1997).

Alexander, Rachel, *Myths, Symbols and Legends of Solar System Bodies* (New York: Springer, 2015).

Alford, Alan F., *The Midnight Sun: The Death and Rebirth of God in Ancient Egypt* (Walsall: Eridu Books, 2004)

Allen, Richard, *Star Names: Their Lore and Meaning* (New York: Dover, 1963).

Annas, Jonathan and Julia Barnes, *Sextus Empiricus' Outlines of Pyrrhonism* (Cambridge: Cambridge University Press, 2002).

Baigent, Michael, *From the Omens of Babylon: Astrology and Ancient Mesopotamia* (London: Arkana, 1994).

Beck, Roger, 'Merkelbach's Mithras' in *Phoenix* vol. 41, no. 3 (Autumn 1987).

Beck, Roger, *The Religion of the Mithras Cult in the Roman Empire: Mysteries of the Unconquered Sun* (Oxford: Oxford University Press, 2006).

Blake, William, *On the Marriage of Heaven and Hell* (Oxford: Oxford University Press, 1975).

Bly, Robert, *A Little Book on the Shadow* (New York: HarperCollins, 1988).

Bly, Robert, *Stealing Sugar From the Castle*, Selected and New Poems, 1950–2013 (W.W. Norton, 2013).

Borsch, Frederick H., *The Son of Man in Myth and History* (Eugene, OR: Wipf & Stock, 2007).

Brady, Bernadette, *Brady's Book of Fixed Stars* (York, ME: Weiser, 1998).

Burke, Vicki, *The Journey to the Golden City: Finding the Way Home* (Leicester: Matador, 2017).

Calasso, Roberto, *The Marriage of Cadmus and Harmony* (London: Vintage, 1994).

Campbell, Alan, *To Square with Genesis, Causal Statements and Shamanic Ideas in Wayapi* (Iowa City: University of Iowa Press, 1989).

Campbell, Joseph, *The Hero with a Thousand Faces* (London: Fontana Press, 1993).

Campion, Nicholas, '*Babylonian Astrology: Its Origin and Legacy in Europe*', in Helaine Selin (ed.), *Astronomy Across Cultures* (London: Kluwer, 2000), pp. 509–553.

Campion, Nicholas, *The Dawn of Astrology: A Cultural History of Western Astrology* (London: Hambledon Continuum, 2008).

Capra, Fritjof, *The Turning Point: Science, Society and the Rising Culture* (New York: Simon & Schuster, 1982).

Capra, Fritjof, *The Web of Life, A New Synthesis of Mind and Matter* (London: Flamingo, 1997).

Clarke, Lindsay, *The Return from Troy* (London: HarperCollins, 2006).

Coleman Smith, Pamela and Arthur Edward Waite, *The Rider Tarot Deck: Known also as The Waite Tarot and the Rider-Waite Tarot* (Stamford: U.S. Games Systems, 1971).

Cornelius, Geoffrey, *The Moment of Astrology: Origins in Divination* (Bournemouth: The Wessex Astrologer, 2003).

Costello, Darby, 'Desire and the Stars', published in *Astrological Journal, vol. 45*, (July/August 2003).

Crane, Beryl, *Reflexology: The Definitive Practitioner's Manual* (HarperCollins UK, 2012).

Crowley, Alesteir, *The Book of Thoth Tarot* (Newburyport, MA: Red Wheel / Weiser, 1981).

Curry, Patrick, 'Magic vs Enchantment', *Journal of Contemporary Religion*, 1999, Vol. 14, no. 3, pp. 401–412.

Devisch, René, *Weaving the Threads of Life, the Khita Gyn-Eco-Logical Healing Cult Among the Yaka* (Chicago: University of Chicago Press, 1993).

Dobin, Rabbi Joel C., *Kabbalistic Astrology: The Sacred Tradition of the Hebrew Sages* (Rochester, VE: Inner Traditions International, 1999).

Einstein, Albert, *Einstein on Cosmic Religion and Other Opinions and Aphorisms* (Mineola, NY: Dover Publications, 2009).

Eliade, Mircea, *The Myth of the Eternal Return* (New Jersey: Princeton University Press, 2005).

Eliade, Mircea, *The Sacred and the Profane: The Nature of Religion* (New York: Harcourt, Brace and World Inc., 1959).

Eliade, Mircea, *Shamanism: Archaic Techniques of Ecstacy* (London: Routledge, 1964).

Fagan, Cyril, *Astrological Origins* (St Paul, MN: Llewellyn, 1971).

Farrah, Janet and Virginia Russell, *The Magical History of the Horse* (London: Robert Hale, 1992).

Ficino, Marsilio (trans. Michael J. Allen), *Platonic Theology,* Vol. 6, Books 17–18 (Cambridge, MA: Harvard University Press, 2006).

Frankfort, Henri A. and Mrs. H. A., John A. Wilson, Thorkild Jacobsen, *Before Philosophy: A Study of the Primitive Myths, Beliefs and Speculations of Egypt and Mesopotamia* (Chicago: University of Chicago Press, 1949).

Frankl, Victor, *Man's Search for Meaning* (Boston, MA: Beacon Press, 2006 [1946]).

Gennep, Arnold van, *The Rites of Passage* (London & New York: Routledge, 2010).

Gleadlow, Rupert, *The Origin of the Zodiac* (New York: Dover Publications, 2011).

Gleadlow, Rupert, *The Zodiac Revealed* (Hollywood, CA: Wilshire, 1972).

Gotschall, Jonathan, *The Storytelling Animal: How Stories Make us Human* (Wilmington, MA: Mariner Books, 2003).

Graves, Robert, *The Greek Myths* (Manchester: Carcanet Press Ltd, 2001 [1955]).

Greene, Liz, *Astrology for Lovers* (San Francisco, CA: Weiser, 1989).

Greene, Liz, *The Astrology of Fate* (York Beach, ME: Weiser, 1984).

Grimm, Jacob Ludwig Carl, *Teutonic Mythology* (Mineola, NY: Dover Phoenix, 2004 [1882]).

Guthrie, W.K.C., *A History of Greek Philosophy* (Cambridge: Cambridge University Press, 1981).

Hamilton, Edith, *Mythology: Timeless Tales of Gods and Heroes* (London: Penguin, 1969).

Harding, Michael, *Hymns to the Ancient Gods* (London: Arkana, 1992).

Harpur, Patrick, *A Complete Guide to the Soul* (London: Rider, 2010).

Harpur, Patrick, *The Philosopher's Secret Fire: A History of the Imagination* (Michigan: Penguin, 2002).

Hay, Peter, *Main Currents in Western Environmental Thought* (Indianapolis, IN: Indiana University Press, 2002).

Heaton, John, 'Pyrrhonean Scepticism: A Therapeutic Phenomenology', *Journal of the British Society for Phenomenology*, 1997, vol. 28, no. 1, pp. 80–96.

Hicks, Esther & Jerry, *The Law of Attraction* (Carlsbad, CA: Hay House, 2006).

Hillman, James, *A Blue Fire* (New York: Harper Perennial, 1989).

Hillman, James, 'Heaven Retains Within Its Sphere Half of All Bodies and Maladies', at http://www.springpub.com/astro.htm [accessed on 15/01/04].

Hillman, James, *The Dream and the Underworld* (New York: Harper & Row, 1979).

Hillman, James, 'Psychology: Monotheistic or Polytheistic?', in David L. Miller (ed.),
    The New Polytheism (Dallas: Spring, 1981).

Hillman, James, *Revisioning Psychology* (New York: Harper Colophon, 1975).

Homer, *The Odyssey* (Boston, MA: Osgood & Co., 1871).

Houlding, Debra, Star Lore of the Constellations at: www.skyscript.co.uk

Hughes, Ted, *Tales from Ovid* (London: Faber & Faber, 1997).

Hutton, Ronald, *The Stations of the Sun: A History of the Ritual Year in Britain* (Oxford:
    Oxford University Press, 1996).

Hyde, Lewis, *Trickster Makes this World: How Disruptive Imagination Creates Culture*
    (Edinburgh: Canongate, 2008).

Hyde, Maggie, *Jung and Astrology* (London: Aquarian, 1992).

Jones, Prudence, *Creative Astrology, Experiential Understanding in the Horoscope*
    (London: Aquarian, 1991).

de Jong, H. M. E, *Michael Maier's Atalanta Fugiens: Sources of an Alchemical Book of
    Emblems* (Berwick, ME: Nicolas-Hays Inc, 2002).

Jung, Carl Gustav., *Collected Works Vol. 9: Aieon*, (Princeton, OR: Princeton University
    Press, 1981).

Jung, Carl Gustav, 'Letter to André Barbault, 26th May, 1954', *Letters* (London: Routledge
    Kegan Paul, 1954).

Jung, Carl Gustav, *Man and His Symbols* (New York: Dell Publishing, 1964).

Kerenyi, Karl, *The Gods of the Greeks* (London and New York: Thames and Hudson,
    1951).

Kerenyi, Karl, *Eleusis: Archetypal Image of Mother and Daughter* (Princeton: Bollingen,
    1967).

Kingsley, Peter, *In the Dark Places of Wisdom* (Inverness, CA: Golden Sufi Center,
    1999).

Klossowski de Rola, Stanslas, *Alchemy: The Secret Art* (New York: Bounty Books,
    1973).

Lietaer, Bernard & Stephen Belgin, *New Money for a New World* (Denver, CO: Qiterra
    Press, 2011).

Long, Charlotte R., *The Twelve Gods of Greece and Rome* (Leiden, NL: E.J. Brill, 1987).

Machado, Antonio, (trans. Robert Bly), *Times Alone: Selected Poems of Antonio
    Machado* (Middletown, CT: Wesleyan; Bilingual Spanish-English ed. 1983).

Mann, A .T., *Astrology and the Art of Healing* (New York, NY: Paraview, 2004).

Mann, A.T., *A New Vision of Astrology: From Conception to Transcendence* (New York: Pocket Books, 2002).

Marlan, Stanton, *The Dark Sun, the Alchemy & Art of Darkness* (Texas: A&M University Press, 2005).

Martineau, John, *A Little Book of Coincidence in the Solar System* (Glastonbury: Wooden Books, 2001).

M'Closkey, Kathy, *Swept Under the Rug: A Hidden History of Navajo Weaving* (Albuquerque, NM: University of New Mexico Press, 2002).

Michell, John & Christine Rhone, *Twelve Tribe Nations and the Science of Enchanting the Landscape* (Grand Rapids, MI: Phanes Press, 1991).

Monaghan, Patricia, (ed.), *Goddesses in World Culture: Vol. I, Asia & Africa* (Santa Barbara, CA: Praeger, 2011).

Monaghan, Patricia, *The Goddess Path: Myths, Invocations & Rituals* (St. Paul, MN: Llewellyn, 2004).

Moore, Thomas, *The Planets Within: The Astrological Psychology of Marsilio Ficino* (Maryland: Lindisfarne Books, 1989).

Moore, Thomas, *The Re-Enchantment of Everyday Life* (New York: Harper Perennial, 1997).

Murphy, G. Ronald., *Tree of Salvation: Yggdrasil and the Cross in the North* (Oxford: Oxford University Press, 2013).

Nietzsche, Frederich, [1879] *The Birth of Tragedy* (Penguin Classics, 2003).

Ovason, David, *The Zelator: A Modern Initiate Explore the Ancient Mysteries* (Newburyport, MA: Weiser, 2000).

Quinodoz, Jean-Michel (trans. David Alcorn), *Reading Freud: A Chronological Exploration of Freud's Writings* (London & New York: Routledge, 2004).

Pagels, Elaine, *The Gnostic Gospels* (New York: Random House, 1989).

Plato, *Timaeus & Critias* (London: Penguin, 1977).

Plunkett, Emmeline, *Calendars & Constellations of the Ancient World* (New York: Cosimo Classics, 2005).

Ptolemy, *Tetrabiblos,* translated by F.E. Robbins (Bury St Edmunds, Suffolk: Loeb Classical Library Harvard University Press, 1940).

Regardie, Israel, *The Golden Dawn: An Account of the Teachings, Rites and Ceremonies of the Order of the Golden Dawn* (Woodbury, MN: Llewellyn Worldwide, 2016).

Reinhart, Melanie, *Chiron: and the Healing Journey*, (London: Penguin, 1990).

Rigoglioso, Margeurite, *The Cult of Divine Birth in Ancient Greece* (New York: Macmillan, 2009).

River, Lindsay and Sally Gillespie, *The Knot of Time: Astrology & Female Experience* (St Paul, MN: Women's Press, 1997).

Rochberg, Francesca, *The Heavenly Writing* (Cambridge: University of Cambridge, 2004).

Sagan, Carl, *The Dragons of Eden: Speculations on the Evolution of Human Intelligence* (New York: Ballantine Books, 1986).

Santillana, Giorgio de and Hertha von Dechend, *Hamlet's Mill: An Essay on Myth and the Frame of Time* (Boston: Nonpareil Books, 1977).

Schermer, Barbara, *Astrology Alive, Experiential Astrology, Astrodrama and the Healing Arts* (Wellingborough: Aquarian, 1989).

Sells, Michael A., *Mystical Languages of Unsaying* (Chicago: University of Chicago Press).

Sharman-Burke, Juliet and Liz Greene, *The Mythic Tarot* (London: Rider, 1989).

Somers, Barbara, *Fires of Alchemy: A Transpersonal Viewpoint* (Shaftesbury: Archive, 2004).

Starbird, Margaret, *The Woman with the Alabaster Jar: Mary Magdalen and the Holy Grail* (Rochester, VT: Bear & Co, 1993).

Stone, Alby, *Wyrd, Fate and Destiny in North European Paganism* (London: self-published, 1989).

Tarnas, Richard, *Cosmos and Psyche* (New York: Plume, 2007).

Thomas, Gail, *Healing Pandora: The Restoration of Hope and Abundance* (Berkeley, CA: North Atlantic Books, 2009).

Thorston, Geraldine, *The Goddess in Your Stars* (New York: Simon & Schuster, 1989).

Twist, Lynne, *The Soul of Money* (New York: Norton, 2003).

Wasson, R. Gordon, Albert Hofmann and Carla P. Ruck, *The Road to Eleusis: Unveiling the Secret of the Mysteries* (Berkeley, CA: North Atlantic Books, 2008).

Williamson, Marianne, *A Return to Love: Reflections on the Principles of 'A Course in Miracles'* (New York: HarperCollins, 1992).

Willis, Roy and Patrick Curry, *Astrology, Science and Culture: Pulling Down the Moon* (Oxford: Berg, 2004).

Witt, R.E., *Isis in the Ancient World* (Ithaca: NY, Cornell University Press, 1971).

Yates, Frances, *The Art of Memory* (Harmondsworth: Penguin, 1978).

Acknowledgements

I have so many people to thank for their inspiration and generous support over the twelve years of developing this work. Inspiring teachers, sponsors, partners, co-workers, students, clients, and friends, who have all contributed in different ways to bringing this work into being. I would like to acknowledge the following people in particular: Chantal Allison, Maggie Bennett, Andreea Bradu, Dr Bernadette Brady, Vicki Burke, Marcia Butchart, Dr Nicholas Campion, Alison Coals, Dr Valerie Cowan, Dr Patrick Curry, Gerard Davies, Mike Dawes, Hazel Hammond, Colette Lassalle, Chrissy Philp, Ben Rayner, Louise Rennison, Lynne Speight, Emma Stow and Dr Anthony Thorley.

And I would like to especially acknowledge the following dear friends for your love, support, insight and encouragement during my process of writing this book: Nadia Alkatabi, Claire Berlyn, Marcia Butchart, Sue Coles, Suzanne Corbie, Flip Dunning, Celia Gunn, Sam Hargreaves, Leo Hawkins, Joanna Hicks, Joseph Hunwick, Brooke Johnson, Jocelyn Jones, Mags Kelly, Tim Knock, John Martineau, Alix Thorpe and Graham Wadsworth.

Thank you also to Dan Goodfellow and Yuri Leitch for your excellent artwork, and to Jeremiah Abrams, Frank Clifford, Suzanne Corbie, Martin Davis, Judy Hall, Sue Hollingsworth, Mark Jones, Tad Mann and Melanie Reinhart for reading through the book and offering your generous endorsements.

And a special thank you to my dear friend and colleague, Anthony Thorley, for partnering me on The Alchemical Journey for the past eight years, for inspiring me, and teaching me so much.

About the author

John's passion for astrology began in 1990, following a profound experience of communion with the night sky, which opened his mind to the poetry of the cosmos and radically altered his worldview. Then, after an intense period of study in his early twenties, he became a full-time professional astrologer.

John has been teaching astrology for many years and is a pioneer in the field of experiential astrological education. He created the Kairos School of Astrology in Glastonbury, which includes a two-year training in the art of birth chart interpretation, and is the founder of 'The Alchemical Journey', the zodiac mystery school upon which this book is based. John holds an MA in Cultural Astronomy & Astrology from Bath Spa University. He also teaches night-sky astronomy and runs a mobile planetarium for schools.